FRIENDSHIP ESTABLISHED

The 'Genesis' of True Friendships

VERITAS PRESS

Veritas Press exists to glorify God by creating truth-centered resources for human flourishing.

Other Veritas Press resources:

Date Different: A Short (but real) Conversation on Dating, Sex, and Marriage for Teenagers (and their parents)

Friendship Redeemed: How the Gospel Changes Friendships to Something Greater

Follow VP on Twitter @Veritas_Press

Purchase from VeritasPress.tv

FRIENDSHIP ESTABLISHED

The 'Genesis' of True Friendships

ADAM HOLLAND

VERITAS PRESS
2016

ISBN-13: 978-0692633809
ISBN-10: 0692633804

Veritas Press Supervising Editor: Greg Gibson

Cover and Layout Design by Mathew B. Sims
www.MathewBryanSims.com

"One may have 5,000 friends on Facebook or another social media outlet, but not have any real friendships in today's world. This is a tragedy given the fact that we are made for relationships. Adam has served the church well by providing a biblical and practical book about the nature and work of Christ-centered friendships. I used it recently in preparing for a sermon, and I'm sure I will turn to it again, for my own benefit, and for the benefit of those that I teach."

TONY MERIDA

Pastor of the Imago Dei Church, Editor of the Exalting Christ in the OT Commentary Series, Associate Professor of Preaching at Southeastern

"Thoughtful, insightful and practical! Holland's book is a probing study of friendship using the book of Genesis, that classic book of beginnings. Particularly helpful is the discussion of the theological basis of friendship and its contemporary application."

STEPHEN DEMPSTER

Author of Dominion and Dynasty Professor of Biblical Studies at Crandall University

"Many in our world are lonely and long for friends, but friendship has to be mapped to the biblical witness so that it is understood in light of the storyline of the scriptures. Holland sets friendship in this biblical context so that our understanding of friendship is rooted in the Bible."

THOMAS R. SCHREINER

James Buchanan Harrison Professor of New Testament Interpretation and Professor of Biblical Theology at Southern Baptist Theological Seminary

"There is nothing like having a friend in a difficult and troubled world. But what does the Bible teach us about friendship? Adam Holland brings the resources available from the book of Genesis to understand and appreciate the nature of true friendship. I recommend this readable and insightful book for all readers."

TREMPER LONGMAN III

Robert H. Gundry Professor of Biblical Studies
Westmont College

"There's a reason we need friends- we were made for them. Adam Holland here, like a friend, instructs and admonishes us on the meaning, importance and calling of friendship, all undergirded with the grace and Word of God."

DR. R.C. SPROUL JR.

Founder of Highlands Ministry, served as the editor and chief of Tabletalk Magazine, Professor at Reformation Bible College and Ligonier Academy, and author.

"Many books have been written about various relationships in the Christian life: parent, child, spouse, employer, etc., but little has been written about friendship, clearly one of the most important relationships we have to other people. Adam Holland's book develops a biblical understanding of friendship, which is where Christians should begin in thinking about the topic. I believe that study of the biblical principles in this volume will enrich these relationships with God's grace, enabling us better to love our neighbors as ourselves."

DR. JOHN FRAME

Professor of Systematic Theology and Philosophy
Reformed Theological Seminary

"Adam's book offers Godly wisdom and biblical insight on building relationships and intentional friendships - a beautiful reminder that we all need each other."

JOSH LOVELACE

keyboardist for NEEDTOBREATHE

"In our dysfunctional world, images of friendship normally emerge either from secular default sources or fantasy works--often lionized in movies, romantic literature, or cheesy songs. This new work is a fresh reminder of more enduring models of friendship--indeed a lost art as well as a theological dynamic. With fine sourcing from the book of Genesis, this work will help recapture some of Eden's lost fruit of friendship. Many churches and families will be helped by this."

DR. DAVID W. HALL

Sr. Pastor Midway Presbyterian (PCA) Church,
Powder Springs, GA.

"Adam Holland has tapped into what I think is a much neglected subject which is the horizontal effects of the Fall and the horizontal healing of the Gospel. His tracing of this two-fold concept throughout the book of Genesis is refreshing and insightful. Adam's sin not only affected his (and our) relationship with God but also his relationship with his fellow image bearer who was also his wife. Holland carefully shows us what was lost in the first Adam and what has been gained in the last Adam. This is a good read; I highly recommend it."

KEN JONES, PASTOR

Glendale Baptist Church
Co-host of White Horse Inn

The topic of friendship is an often-overlooked subject both in theory and in practice. As I read this book, I was reminded of how vital the practice of being a friend is and challenged with how much I need to grow in my own friendships. May this book do the same work in you, calling you to display the gospel by how you walk in love with others.

MATT BOSWELL

Pastor of Ministries and Worship, Providence Church, Frisco,
Texas, President, Doxology & Theology

"Adam Holland has done the church a tremendous service in writing this book on friendship, an under-explored concept in recent Christian publishing. Basing much of his exposition on narratives in Genesis, Holland carefully crafts what can only be called both a theology and a technology of Christian friendship. He draws from some of the best theological resources in Christian history: Augustine, Thomas Aquinas, Calvin, Luther, William Carey, Charles Spurgeon, Dietrich Bonhoeffer and many others, all of whom had a deep understanding of "friendship." I heartily recommend this book to pastors, students, and laymen alike as both a corrective and a guide to this very important subject."

CHAD OWEN BRAND

Adjunct Professor of Apologetics,
Oklahoma Baptist University, and Pastor in Crossville, TN

"Like an alarm, Holland seeks to awake a sleeping church to its need for Christ in their friendships. I pray God will use this book to bring the gospel back to its rightful place. This book will help you make much of Christ in your relationships."

JOHNNY HUNT

Pastor of Woodstock Baptist Church and
former President of the SBC

To my wife and best friend Katelyn, who
constantly gives me a visual definition of the
word "friend."
I would also like to dedicate this book to Dr. Brian
Payne, who showed me how all of scripture
proclaims Christ.

TABLE OF CONTENTS

Introduction   *15*

THE BEGINNING OF FRIENDSHIP

Chapter I. Friendship Established   23
    Friendship Broken   26
    Friendship Restored   34

THE MISSION OF FRIENDSHIP

Chapter II. The Mission of Friendship   55
    "Mission Impossible"   59
    Mission Accomplished   65

IDENTITY IN FRIENDSHIP

Chapter III. Identity in Friendship   77
    Identity Established & Broken   78
    Identity Restored   85
Chapter IV. God's Word in Friendship   91
    The Word Established & Word Fallen   93

God's Word Restored 98

Chapter V. Prayer in the Garden Temple 109
    Prayer Established & Fallen 110
    Prayer Restored 115

About the Author *127*

INTRODUCTION

Friendship is something that we all experience in life. Our friendships begin in the nursery and end all the way at our deathbeds. Friends are with us through all of life's joys and struggles. Friendship is at the heart of who we are as created beings. C.S. Lewis describes friendship as "having no survival value, rather it is one of those things which gives value to survival." Our friendships enrich our lives. Without friendship Lewis rightfully explains, life would truly lack luster and joy. Since friendships have existed since the creation of man, why write a second book on the topic? Shouldn't we be experts on the issue by now? Although we all have friendships and participate in them regularly most of us miss their purpose, mission, and goal.

Friendships were not created as a result of the fall of man. Friendships also weren't something extra that have no value or point. Friendships weren't a side item on the local value meal. They are not something you add on at the end or upgrade to for 75 cents more. Friendships are tied to the purpose and mission of mankind. The way in which God's mission is accomplished in the world is through friendships. The goal of this book is to help the reader reclaim and return their friendships to their intended purpose and goal.

I want to begin at the offset saying that this book is not claiming that after you read it you will have "Your Best Friendships Now." This is not a self-help book on friendships. You will not get a "ten step guide" with this book. The goal of this book is to examine the topic of friendship through the lens of scripture and more specifically through the book of Genesis. I want to bring up that I am not claiming with this book to have perfect relationships. Also, let me say at the forefront that I often will "write above my own sanctification."[1] After reading this book you may find your friendships are not easier, but actually more difficult than before. When a friendship returns to its God intended purpose, things often become more difficult. Even though your friendships may be more difficult, this does not mean that they will not be more satisfying or enriching. Faithfulness and delight in the Lord are never achieved by a life of ease. Friendship demands certain things in order for it to accomplish its goal and purpose. These things sin

---

[1] A phrase I borrowed from Dr. Brian Payne.

and Satan desire to wreak havoc on, thus preventing friendship from accomplishing its intended purpose. With this book I want to examine several core tenets of friendship. If we desire to grow in our friendships we must constantly look to these tenets over and over again. Because of sin, we are like recovering drug addicts. We are constantly fighting against the desire to relapse into a life of ease. Sin desires to ruin our friendships. When you do relapse, my hope is that this book will provide you a place to constantly return to find a firm foundation. Where is this firm foundation? When waves come and toss you to and fro, the only place you will find security will be in the rock of Jesus Christ. This brings me to the theme of the book: how the gospel transforms.

The gospel is "THE TURNING POINT" in all of history. All of scripture speaks of and testifies to Christ. It is through this lens that I write this book. This book is setup with this truth in mind. I strive to begin every chapter in the book of Genesis and end every chapter with Christ. I also strive to show how different aspects of friendship were created, how sin caused their demise, and finally how the gospel transforms/restores these aspects of friendship. Part of the good news of the finished work of Jesus Christ is that God is restoring all things to their intended purpose under the headship of Christ (Ephesians 1:9-10). This is the hope for friendships, that through the gospel they can recover their intended purpose. I have always enjoyed the way Michael Horton began his phenomenal book Christless Christianity. Horton begins his book by telling the story of a radio interview that once took place with Donald Barnhouse. The radio host asked Barnhouse, "What would a city look like if it was ruled by Satan?" Barnhouse's response has stuck with me ever since I first read it in 2008. Barnhouse responds by saying,

> *What would things look like if Satan really took control of a city?" Barnhouse speculated "all of the bars would be closed. pornography banish, and pristine streets would be filled with tidy pedestrians who smiled at each other. There would be no swearing. The children would say, "Yes, sir" and "No, ma'am," and the churches would be full every Sunday... where Christ is not preached.*[2]

I wrestled with this quote for the longest time. Barnhouse is incredibly helpful in showing how what so many Christians think is Christianity is simply a glorified moralism. Christ did not come to make us moralistic self-righteous people. Christ came to show us our sinfulness and our need of a

---

[2] Donald Barnhouse, "Quoted in Michael Horton's *Christless Christianity:The Alternative Gospel of the American Church* (Grand Rapids: Mi, Baker Books Publishing, 2008), 15.

savior. Christ is the long awaited promised seed of Eve (Genesis 3:15), who came to redeem the world by his sacrificial death. Christ then sends His Spirit and thus transforms everything. My desire is that God will use this book to transform your friendships. May our friendships declare Christ's reign over all things.

THE BEGINNING OF FRIENDSHIPS

"There is nothing on this earth more to be prized than true friendship."
– Thomas Aquinas

"Then the LORD God said, "It is not good that the man should be alone..."
– Genesis 2:18

"In this world two things are essential: life and friendship. Both should be highly prized and we must not undervalue them."
– Augustine of Hippo

"He who would be happy here must have friends; and he who would be happy hereafter, must, above all things, find a friend in the world to come, in the person of God, the Father of his people."
– Charles Spurgeon

FRIENDSHIP
ESTABLISHED

It was the bottom of the 5th inning, the third game of the World Series, and the score was tied. The count at the plate was two balls and two strikes. The batter stepped back up to the plate. All seemed to be normal until the batter pointed toward the centerfield wall. The pitcher wound-up and threw the ball. The batter swings and the crowd went wild. The ball sailed over the centerfield wall. This exchange has become one of the most famous plays in all of sports history.

Fast-forward now about fifty years. Every child playing backyard baseball at some point has now repeated this same action. Whether it be to antagonize the pitcher or simply as a display of confidence, every child longs to repeat this scene. Children everywhere step up to the plate and point to the outfield wall and then they swing for the fence. Not all have been as successful in fulfilling this claim as Babe Ruth. Babe Ruth's famous "calling his shot" changed backyard baseball forever.

Just like many things in life, repeated actions often lose their historic significance. Most children when "calling their shot" do not realize that the action that they are repeating took place originally by Babe Ruth and in one of the last games of the World Series. Adding to the significance of the event, most do not realize that the series ended with the Yankees sweeping the Cubs and Lou Gehrig, not Babe Ruth being the team's best hitter through the series.[3] When children repeat this action, what they fail to realize is that they are repeating one of, if not the most significant plays in all of sports history. Actions lose their value through negligence and ignorance of their purpose and origin. This negligence is not only true with baseball and "calling a shot," but it is also true of friendship.

Friendship is something that we all experience in life. Because it is something that we all experience so regularly, we often overlook its origin and purpose. Much like the children playing backyard ball, calling their shot, the history of their action has no meaning or value to them. The greatest experience and joy is reserved

---

[3]The information that I gathered about this event came from the following source: http://www.baseball-almanac.com/ws/yr1932ws.shtml

for the diehard fans, who appreciate not only the "calling of the shot" but also the significance of all the events surrounding it. Similarly the great joys and experiences in friendship are reserved for those, who understand its origin, purpose, and mission. So, where were friendships established and what are their purposes?

Man was created as a relational being. God, prior to creating the universe, was in perfect relationship within the godhead. Upon creating the earth, scripture then tells us that God created man in his image. Just as God was relational, so was man created to be relational. Man was created to reflect the perfect unity that existed with God in eternity. This reality comes to the forefront when God was creating the universe.

God first creates the heavens and the earth and declares that they are "GOOD". God then creates and separates the day from the night. God declares that they too are "GOOD". When the reader comes to Genesis 2:18, the reader encounters something new, the Lord says that something is "NOT GOOD." God declares that it is "NOT GOOD" for man to be alone. Relationships were created prior to the Fall of man. Relationships were not something that was deemed necessary after man had sinned and the curses were placed upon them. Relationships were not a result of the Fall. Relationships were created before sin ever entered into the world.

When we take this concept and apply it to our lives we realize we were created to be in relation with other people. Man was created with a need for friendship. Man was created in perfect relationship with each other, but also with God himself. An easy way to remember this is that we were created in perfect relation both vertically and horizontally. To illustrate this we only need two perpendicular lines. The vertical line represents man's relationship with God. The horizontal line represents man's relationship with the rest of humanity.

There were no problems, but only perfect communion with both relationships. It is not until sin enters into the picture that these relationships become divided.

Man's relationship with God

Man's relationship with fellow man.

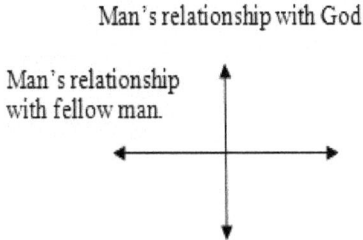

FRIENDSHIP BROKEN

Adam and Eve
Man after being placed in the Garden of Eden was tempted to not take the Lord at his word. After

choosing to trust the serpent rather than the Lord, sin enters into the world. The very first thing that happens after sin enters into the world is that it separates man from woman and man from God. No longer was there the perfect unity that existed both vertically and horizontally.

Man and woman both seek out clothing to cover themselves. Man and woman then hide themselves when they hear the Lord coming in the Garden. God does not leave man here without hope. God promises man that one day there will be a seed from the line of Eve that will crush the head of the serpent. This seed will restore all that was lost from the Garden of Eden. Friendship with man and God will one day be restored to its perfect state. Although God provides hope to mankind, there are still consequences for the sin which they committed.

The way in which sin works in the lives of people today is the same way in which it worked then. Sin works itself out by pulling people away from others and pulling people away from the Lord. Tim Chester in his book A Meal with Jesus diagnoses the state of our modern culture demonstrating sin's power to separate by saying,

> *We protect ourselves from outsiders, but our security systems and garden gates are prisons, cutting us off from community. Instead we get our community vicariously through soap operas. Friends is a television*

program or a Facebook number, not the people with whom we eat and laugh and cry.[4]

Rather than people experiencing true friendship and the fellowship which they were created for, people set up barriers to further separate themselves from others. The serpent's scheme is still working today. As a result of these barriers or walls, genuine friendship becomes more and more difficult to experience. Robert Putman, a professor of Public Policy at Harvard University, verifies this reality of the decline of friendship and fellowship in his book Bowling Alone by saying,

> *In the mid-to late 1970s, according to the DDB Needham Style archive, the average American entertained friends at home about fourteen to fifteen times a year. By the late 1990s that figure had fallen to eight times per year, a decline of 45 percent in barely two decades. An entirely independent series of surveys from the Roper Social and Political Trends archive confirms that both going out to see friends and having them*

---

[4] Tim Chester, A Meal with Jesus: Discovering Grace, Community, and MIssion around the Table (Wheaton: Il, Crossway Publishing Company, 2011), 46.

over to our home declined from the mid-1970s to the mid-1990s.[5]

The separation that occurred as a result of the Fall even today still continues its path of destruction in our relationships. The separation that began in the Garden of Eden continues to grow as the reader progresses through the book of Genesis.

Cain and Abel

What started off as one sin in the Garden further progressed in the next generation. Shortly after the fall Adam and Eve have two children: Cain and Abel. Both children bring an offering to the Lord. The reader is told that the Lord was pleased with Abel's offering, but not with Cain's. This resulted in Cain being furious with Abel. The Lord confronts Cain, similarly to how He confronted Adam and Eve in the Garden. The Lord asks Cain, "Why are you angry?" The Lord then gives Cain a warning and tells him, "Sin is crouching at the door; and its desire is for you, but you must master it."

Bruce Waltke an Old Testament scholar is helpful in tying the story of Cain and Abel back to the Garden of Eden when he says, "The depiction

---

[5] Robert D. Putman, Bowling Alone: The Collapse and Revival of American Community (New York: New York, Simon and Schusters Publishing Company, 2000), 98.

of sin as a demon or a vicious animal lying in wait to devour is possibly an allusion to the serpent waiting to strike the heel."[6] Just as the serpent desired to separate, he is once again on the prowl seeking to bring more division among humanity. Sydney Griedanus reiterates this idea, but shows even further how the serpent and sin strive to separate man from God and the rest of humanity when he says,

> *The serpent is ready to strike again in the second generation. This time he tempts Cain the firstborn. God warns Cain, 'Do well.' But Cain refuses to listen to God; instead he nurses his anger at God and his jealousy of his brother Abel.*[7]

Rather than repenting and trusting the Lord and restoring fellowship with the Lord and Abel, Cain follows after his father the serpent. Cain kills Abel. Jesus ties the story of Cain and Abel to the serpent of the Garden as well, demonstrating that sin and the serpent have since the beginning devised to prevent man from accomplishing his

---

[6] Bruce Waltke, Genesis: A Commentary (Grand Rapids: Mi, Zondervan Publishing Company, 2001), 98.

[7] Sidney Greidanus, Preaching Christ from Genesis: Foundations for Expository Sermons (Grand Rapids: Mi, William B. Eerdmans Publishing Company, 2007), 94.

created purpose. Jim Hamilton explains this quiet well saying, "When Jesus said that Satan was 'a murderer from the beginning.' (John 8:44), he was almost certainly referring to Cain killing Abel. Then John speaks of the 'children of the devil' who are 'like Cain, who was of the evil one and murdered his brother' (1 John 3:10, 12)."[8] Within one generation sin progressed from "shame" to "murder." Sin works in modern friendships the same way. What may start off as a simple transgression against a brother, left unforgiven or unrepentant of often will separate or end a friendship. Sin did not end its destruction with Cain and Abel, it only continued to progress.

Noah
When the reader comes to Genesis 6 he hears that rather than the earth being filled with the knowledge and glory of the Lord, it is now filled with evil and corruption. The divide between man's relationship with God and others has grown even further. God then looked down upon the earth and saw its corruption. God decided that He will destroy the earth and start anew. God in mercy determined that he would save Noah and his family from this cosmic destruction. God destroyed the entire earth with a flood. Afterwards God gives

---

[8] James M. Hamilton, God's Glory in Salvation Through Judgment (Wheaton, IL, 2010), 83.

Noah the same command or mission in which He gave Adam.

Just as God commissioned Adam and Eve to "be fruitful and multiple and fill the earth (Gen 1:28)", so He also commissioned Noah with the same task. Noah is called to start-over acting as a type of Adam. Noah must start-over from scratch establishing a new humanity. Noah's father, Lamech believed his son would be the promised seed of Eve, the one who will bring the long awaited resolve. Lamech names his child Noah or "Out of the ground that the Lord has cursed, this one shall bring us relief." The curse of the ground, which Lamech is referring would have drawn the original audience and should also draw the modern reader back to the curse, which God placed on Adam and Eve because of the first sin. Will friendship with God and friendship with fellow man find its resolve with the birth of this child? Stephen Dempster answers this question saying, "Noah fails like the old one (Adam) as a result of fruit taken from a vine instead of a tree."[9] Just as Adam falls by the fruit of the tree, so Noah falls by the fruit of the vine. What was supposed to be the re-establishment of a new humanity with Noah failed once again. Sin once again continued to progress after Noah.

---

[9] Stephen Dempster, Dominion and Dynasty: A Theology of the Hebrew Bible (Downers Grove: Il, InterVarsity Press, 2003), 73.

Tower of Babel

Genesis 11 begins with all of God's people being united with one language. The people of Babel determine to build a city that reaches the heavens. Moses explains their reasoning for doing so was "to make a name for themselves." Rather than filling the earth with the glory of God, the people of Babel sought to build up their own kingdom. Rather than making much of God, they desired to make much of themselves. William VanGemeren describes this scene saying,

> In Genesis 11 humanity becomes wickedly united in its defiance of the Creator. God decreed to make humans in his image, saying 'let us make..' (1:26). At Babel, however, humans use the same expression ('let us make...'; 11:3) to seek to displace God's glory with their own glory.[10]

As a result of their sin God separated man and divided their language. The language which was created for the purpose of building up, encouraging one another, and ultimately

---

[10] Willem VanGemeren, Gospel Transformation Study Bible, study notes from Genesis (Wheaton:Il, Crossway Book Publishing Company, 2013) ,17.

bringing the Lord glory has now been confused because of sin. There is now a barrier that makes friendship and relationships even more difficult. The ramifications of this event continue to have lasting effects. You may be able to think of a situation where you long to communicate with someone, but have been prevented from doing so because of language. Once again because of sin there is an even greater divide within mankind. Is there any hope for restoration?

FRIENDSHIP RESTORED

It was the beginning of what would be a brutal war. World War I would undoubtedly change the course of history. Several months into the war there were pleas for a momentary truce for the upcoming holidays. Troops on all sides had been engaged in battle for over 4 months. Christmas Eve had arrived and along a 27 mile trench everything seemed as a normal battle day. As night approached, the sound of gunfire slowly changed into an unusual noise. Soldiers began singing Christmas carols. Candles were placed upon trees. Soldiers went into enemy territory and exchanged gifts, cigarettes, and showed everyone pictures of their families. At one point during the day a soccer game took place between enemy forces. There was even a report of a chocolate cake being snuck in and shared among the soldiers. As the Christmas holiday came to a close, the men went their separate ways and the shots began to fire once again.[11] This act is definitely an incredible display of humanity, generosity, and love in the midst of a terrible war. But this act can also teach us something about forgotten purpose.

When a soldier is enlisted into war, he is enlisted with a purpose. The purpose of a soldier is to complete the mission of his king and his kingdom. Removing the "Christmas Truce" story away from its romanticism, we can see an example of soldiers who forgot their purpose. When people forget their purpose, they risk of compromising their mission. In order for our friendships to fulfill their intended purpose, man's relationship with God must first be restored.

---

[11] The information that I gathered about this event came from the following sources:

http://militaryhistory.about.com/od/worldwari/p/xmastruce.htm

http://www.history.com/topics/world-war-i/christmas-truce-of-1914

http://www.firstworldwar.com/features/christmastruce.htm

Christ's redemptive work
restores man's relationship with God

Adam and Eve

The Fall of man occurred because man sinned against God first. Afterwards man's relationship with each other went haywire. The restoration must take place in the same order if we desire our friendships to fulfill their intended purpose. Hear me out. I am not saying that in order for a person to have friendships or even experience joy in friendship, he must be a Christian. What I am saying is that the greatest joys in friendship are reserved for those, who have a restored relationship with the Lord. Any relationship that does not find its root in reconciliation to the Lord will miss the ultimate purpose of friendship. Adam and Eve were created with a purpose. Adam and Eve were called to "be fruitful and multiple and fill the earth." If Adam and Eve had been faithful, they would have taken what was true in the Garden and extended it until the whole earth was filled with the knowledge of the glory of the Lord (Habakkuk 2:14).

FRIENDSHIP ESTABLISHED

Adam and Eve failed, but God did not leave them without hope. Who would be the promised seed, who restores both God's relationship with man and with God? When the reader turns to the New Testament, one of the first things he encounters is a genealogy of a "seed." Could this be the promised seed of Genesis 3:15? Matthew cites the angel of the Lord tying Jesus' birth to Isaiah 7 saying, "you shall call him 'Immanuel', which means "God with us." Matthew then concludes and bookends his gospel by showing how Christ fulfills this promise. Matthew ends with Jesus saying, "I am with you always." The sin which once separated God from man has now been crushed. Christ comes and restores the relationship that was lost with God. Furthermore, Christ brings the image of God to man. The relationship that existed with God in eternity, which Adam and Eve failed to reflect, Christ has come and restored. Paul explains this reality by telling us that "he (Jesus) is the image of the invisible God (Col 1:15)." Because Christ has restored man's relationship with God, man's reconciliation with fellow man is now possible.

←————→

Christ's redemptive work
restores the divide among human relationships.

Cain and Abel

Adam and Eve's sin resulted in shame and separation. From that point on sin only progressed in further separating man. The next generation displayed sin's brutal ability to destroy relationships. Cain, acting like the seed of the serpent, kills his brother Abel. When it seems like Satan has won and ruined all hope for true friendship to exist, God makes a way. When it seemed like Satan had won by killing Abel, God provided another seed. Seth was born. A similar tension occurs in the New Testament. Satan seems to have won the battle when the promised seed (Jesus) is put to death. Christ is then raised defeating death. It is this defeat that brings hope for humanity to restore man's relationship with one another. Paul once again shows us how this relates to our relationships with one another.

Paul's begins his letter to the Ephesians explaining how God's plan to fix the relationship problems was by "summing up of all things in Christ (Ephesians 1:10)." Paul then explains how this summing up or restoration was taking place. The restoration of all things is being accomplished through the gospel (Ephesians 2). We were all once alienated from God because of our sin, but then God displayed grace to us through the cross. In chapter 4 Paul then gives believers implications of this new life in Christ. Paul tells the Ephesian believers to walk in a manner that is worthy of their calling.

Afterwards, he tells them what this looks like. Paul says,

> *"With all humility and gentleness, with patience, bearing with one another in love, eager to maintain the unity of the Spirit in the bond of peace. There is one body and one Spirit—just as you were called to the one hope that belongs to your call— one Lord, one faith, one baptism, one God and Father of all, who is over all and through all and in all (Eph. 4:2-5)."*

Those who have been redeemed by Christ are called to be unified. Sin separated. Christ came to restore and bring unity. Paul gives as an example of our unity, the oneness of God. Believers are called to be one because God is one. Furthermore, the relationships among believers give testimony to the fact that God is restoring everything to its intended purpose. Friendship then is not the gospel, but gives testimony to its reality. This truth has many implications that come along with it.

Christians are saved to be in relationships. Steve Wilkins explains this well when he says, "God, in His mercy, does not save us in isolation from other people but rather in community with other people. If we are to be all that God commands us to be, we must realize that having godly relationships with friends is vital to the whole process."[12] Man was not created to be alone. It was only after the fall that this perfect unity was broken. What sin separated once again Christ has brought back together. Although it may sound "spiritual", the concept "that it is just me and God and that I do not need anyone" is foreign to the Bible. N.T. Wright in his book Simply Christian shows how the Christian concept of unity and fellowship is foreign to our modern society saying,

> *Many people today find it difficult to grasp this sense of corporate Christian identity. We have been so soaked in the individualism of modern western culture that we feel threatened by the idea of our primary identity being a family we belong to... The church isn't simply a collection of isolated individuals, all following their own pathways of spiritual growth without much reference to one another.[13]*

Christians have been saved to be in fellowship with one another. Christians are called to: love one another, honor one another, greet

---

[12] Steve Wilkins, Face to Face: Mediations on Friendship and Hospitality (Moscow: Id 2002), 11.

[13] N.T. Wright, Simply Christian (New York: New York, Harper Collins Publishing Company, 2006), 203.

one another, serve one another, bear with one another, submit to one another, forgive one another, encourage one another, show mercy and justice to one another, and etc. These callings demand that we live life together. These things cannot be done in isolation. Christian friendship is a central part of the Christian life. Christ's death crushes the head of the serpent and restores the fellowship that was lost in the garden. The story of Cain and Abel demonstrate to us that sin leads to death. Cain and Abel were called to reflect the relationship which existed with God. Rather than reflect that relationship Cain gives in to sin's temptation. Sin has its natural progression and brings forth death. James reaffirms this idea with an analogy. James says sin gives birth to a child and that child is death. James tells the readers that sin leads to death, but that is not the end of the story.

Noah

James does not leave the reader without hope. Sin giving birth to a child, which was death, was not the end. Adam and Eve were given the task to establish humanity. Adam and Eve's sin led to death. Noah then was called to establish a new humanity, one which would reflect the image of God (Gen 9:7). Noah failed at the establishing a new humanity. James then continues on with his analogy and says that God, through his word, brings forth life or a new humanity (James 1:18).

FRIENDSHIP ESTABLISHED

Because of the finished work of Christ, a new humanity has been established. What Adam and Noah failed to accomplished, God has accomplished through Christ. Jesus comes and tells man that they must be born again in order to experience the kingdom of God. Christians are called to live as people whose lives are set in a new kingdom. What will ultimately be true in the New Jerusalem, Christians are called to reflect now through their lives and relationships. This new humanity is characterized by its love for others (James 2:8, John 13:34-35).

The love and relationships that are typified in the New Testament are not the casual acquaintances. The relationships that are described in the New Testament are relationships that have deep roots, that forgive liberally, and that carry each others' burdens. This is not the person you shake hands with only during the "meet and greet" time during your Sunday gathering. This is also not the small group that you really never live life together with. Tim Keller writing about community describes accurately the relationships/friendships that the New Testament calls for when he says,

> *Christians expect to find community by attending church services and coming to a small group....it is possible to hold a weekly small group meeting without adding the elements that create real community.*

FRIENDSHIP ESTABLISHED

Because of our idols and the habits of our heart church events simply become places that individuals 'focus on themselves in the presence of others.' It takes deep reflection and costly commitment to live in community.[14]

Quality friendship does not come naturally. Sin and Satan are prowling around seeking to destroy and further divide people from one another. What Satan came to destroy, Christ came to transform. The friendships to which we are called to are ones that are transformed by Christ's finished work. Dietrich Bonheoffer in his classic *Life Together* explains the beginning of the gospel transformed friendship by saying, "Our community with one another consists solely in what Christ has done to both of us."[15] The gospel is the very thing that restores man to man and man to God. Therefore, the gospel must be at the heart of true friendship.

The gospel brings friendship to a new level. Bonheoffer once again is helpful in showing how the gospel calls for a greater friendship when he

---

[14] Timothy Keller, *Gospel in Life: Grace Changes Everything* (Grand Rapids: Mi, Zondervan Publishing, 2010), 56.

[15] Dietrich Bonheoffer, *Life Together: The Classic Exploration in Community* (New York: New York, Harper Collins Publishing Company, 1954), 25.

says, "I can no longer condemn or hate a brother for whom I pray, no matter how much trouble he causes me. His face, that hitherto may have been strange and intolerable to me, is transformed in intercession into countenance of a brother for whom Christ died, the face of a forgiven sinner."[16] The secular friendship forgives when it benefits the forgiver. For the Christian, forgiveness is rooted in the reality that we have been forgiven in Christ; therefore we too are called to forgive others. Jesus illustrates this with this parable of the debtor.

Peter comes to Jesus and asks him, how often he should forgive someone who has sinned against him. Peter asks, "seven times?" Jesus responds by saying, "I do not say to you seven times, but seventy-seven times." Jesus is not giving an arbitrary number that once Peter meets he can stop forgiving. Jesus clarifies this with his illustration of a debtor who has been forgiven of a great debt by his master. Afterwards, this forgiven debtor fails to forgive a person who owes him a little debt. The master then returns and is furious with his servant because he failed to forgive a little debt, when he had been forgiven of a great debt. The new humanity which Christ came to establish is one which is characterized by radical forgiveness. Are you a friend, who others would consider to be a radical forgiver? Christ

---

[16] Ibid, 86.

came to forgive you of a great debt so that you can forgive others when they transgress against you. The way in which you reflect the image of God and demonstrate that God is restoring all things to their intended purposes is through demonstrating radical forgiveness. The only way to make sense of a friendship that reflects this quality is by the gospel. Another characteristic of this new humanity is sharing all of life together.

Tower of Babel

The people of Babel wanted to make a name for themselves rather than making much of the name of the Lord (Genesis 11:4). God responds to their actions by saying,

> *"Behold, they are <u>one people</u>, and they have all <u>one language</u>, and this is only the beginning of what they will do. And nothing that they propose to do will now be impossible for them. Come, let us go down and there confuse their language, so that they may not understand one another's speech (Genesis 11:6-7)."*

As a result of man's sins, God further separates man by confusing their language. When the reader turns to the New Testament, the first major event he encounters after the resurrection is the Day of Pentecost. Luke uses

45

similar language to what was used at the Tower of Babel. The people are once again gathered together as "one people." These people were not gathered together to build their own kingdom, but were gather together to advance the kingdom of God. Once again the people are speaking in many languages, but the Spirit performs a transforming work. Where Babel brought division, the gospel once again restores. At Babel everyone was speaking different languages and it brought confusion. At Pentecost everyone is speaking different languages but the Spirit brings about understanding and unity. This unity does not end at Pentecost. The rest of the book of Acts gives testimony of believers gathering together as "one" regularly for prayer, fellowship, and the God's word (e.g., Acts 2:42, 2:46, 4:32-36, 20:11). How does this impact and inform our friendships?

When the gospel transforms a friendship, it is only natural for friends to starting sharing life with one another. The gospel transformed friendship reflects the reality that God is restoring all things under the headship of Christ. It accomplishes this task by Christians sharing all of life together. What sin has separated once again Christ has brought back together. The early church exemplified this by their sharing of their time and goods. John Frame in his book Doctrine of the Christian Life describes the lifestyles of the early church when he says,

FRIENDSHIP ESTABLISHED

Fellowship is having in common; it is sharing something with someone else. In the New Testament, it sometimes means sharing goods...They shared their hearts they shared their souls, and they shared their property. Some of the Christians sold property and gave the proceeds to the apostles for needs of fellow Christians. That is a kind of fellowship we rarely see in the church today, but it is simply an expression of the love that Jesus taught us. He told us to love one another as he loved us. That means being ready to lay down your life for another Christian.[17]

The gospel transformed friendship calls for believers spending time together, sharing their hearts with one another, sacrificing for one another. This looks like friends going to a coffee shop and spending a hour or so together talking about life and the Lord. Put your cell phones away and enjoy each other's presence.

Although cell phones have made it possible for us to do much more than any generation may have been able to do in the past, they also have hurt our fellowship. Will Ferrell referring to marriage wittily stated, "Before you get married

---

[17] John M. Frame, The Doctrine of the Christian Life (Phillipsburg: New Jersey, P & R Publishing Company, 2008), 921.

ask yourself: Is this the person you want to watch stare at their phone the rest of your life?"[18] I cannot tell you how many times I have witnessed this scene played in restaurants or local coffee shops. People will often get together and spend almost the entire time staring at their phones. I have a good friend, who has even named this type of scene. When people get together and stare at their phones the entire time, he describes them as having "glowface" (i.e., this in reference to the afterglow from their cell phones). Satan desires to even ruin the time we have organized to get together for fellowship. Satan has managed to separate man even when they are gathered together. Make an effort to put your phones away and enjoy each other's presence. Frame noted a key aspect missing from our friendships that was present among the early church was the sharing of their property.

The secular world calls for people to use their income in order to build their own kingdom. The gospel calls believers to use their finances with a kingdom purpose. God has not blessed you with your finances in order for you only to keep them to yourself. God provides you with your finances in order for you to advance his kingdom. So, how should finances be used within friendship to better advance the kingdom of God?

---

[18] Quoted from Will Ferrell's twitter account @Will__Ferrell

FRIENDSHIP ESTABLISHED

In the next chapter we will examine how gospel transformed friendships fuel mission. We should use our finances to strengthen, encourage, and help other believers. One example of this from scripture is when the church of Philippi sent Epaphroditus with finances in order to strengthen Paul when he was imprisoned in Rome. Epaphroditus acts as a friend and a financial support for Paul during his missionary journey. The gospel takes what was once used to establish and build your own kingdom and makes it common among the believers. The early church was not promoting socialism, but advocating a life that places the advancement of God's kingdom above all things. This may look different for every family or person. The point being is that gospel transformed friendship uses finances to build up, help, encourage, and also fuel mission. We will dive into this further in the next chapter.

APPLICATION

1. What is the purpose of friendship? (Discuss)

2. In what ways can you better reflect the image of God in your friendships? (Discuss)

3. What role does the gospel play in changing our friendships? (Discuss)

4. How does the New Testament describe the new humanity Christ has come to establish? Over the next month what are some things that you can do to better reflect this reality? (Discuss)

5. How can you use your finances to better serve your friendships? (Discuss)

6. Plan over the next few weeks to go sit with a friend for an hour or two and talk about life, your family, and the Lord. (Plan)

7. Plan a get together with a group of people to play a game (e.g., Texas Holdem, board, etc.). Have everyone plan to discuss a theological issue. Have fun and talk about the Lord. (Plan)

8. Read Ephesians 4

THE MISSION OF FRIENDSHIP

"The church exists by mission, just as fire exists by burning."
– Emil Brunner

"The Gospel is a fact, therefore tell it simply; it is a joyful fact, therefore tell it cheerfully; it is an entrusted fact, therefore tell it faithfully; it is a fact of infinite moment, therefore tell it earnestly; it is a fact about a Person, therefore preach Christ."
– Archibald G. Brown
(Spurgeon's Successor)

"A young man should ask himself not if it is his duty to go to the heathen, but if he may dare stay at home. The command is so plain: 'Go.'"
– Lottie Moon

Go therefore and make disciples of all nations, baptizing them in the name of the Father and of the Son and of the Holy Spirit, teaching them to observe all that I have commanded you.
– Matthew 28:19-20

THE MISSION OF FRIENDSHIP

Most people have never heard of Magnus Carlsen. Carlsen was born in 1990 in Tonsberg, Norway. Carlsen began to display an intellectual prowess when he was only two years old. At the age of two Carlsen was able to put together fifty piece puzzles. By the time he was five years old Carlsen was already putting together Lego sets that were created for young teens. When Carlsen was only five years old, his father taught him how to play the game of chess. When Carlsen was only thirteen years old he became the youngest grandmaster of chess.[19] Carlsen recently made headlines for beat-

---

[19] Simen Agdestein, *Wonderboy Magnus Carlsen: How Magnus Carlsen Became the Youngest Grandmaster in the World* (Alkmaar: Netherlands, New in Chess Publishing Company, 2004), 1-10.

ing Bill Gates the founder of Microsoft in a little over a minute.[20] Carlsen was believed to be the greatest chess player to ever live, even before he was out of his teenage years.

I enjoy playing chess. I do not recall when I first started playing or who taught me how to play. I am also not from any exotic location similar to that of Norway. I once lost to a guy in three moves. If I was completely honest, I have lost to this person multiple times with three moves. I have never been amazing at chess, but I do enjoy playing it. The thing that intrigues me about chess is that the strategy of the game. There are always situations where you think you have to outwit your opponent only to find out four moves later that it was just a setup to defeat you. When we come to scripture we experience a similar scenario.

In scripture the reader gets to experience something similar to a divine chess match. Ever since the Garden the serpent has constantly tried to outwit the Lord. What Satan fails to realize throughout scripture is that every move which he feels like he is making a forward advance, is only a move that is setting him up for a future defeat. After God created Adam and Eve, He gave them a mission. Adam and Eve were called to "be fruitful and multiple and fill the earth." The mission was

---

[20] http://www.nydailynews.com/news/world/world-chess-champ-beats-bill-gates-80-seconds-article-1.1591720

tied to their relationship. The mission could not be completed apart from that relationship. Adam and Eve were called to take what was true in the Garden and extend its boundaries to the entire earth. Greg Beale in his book *Temple and the Church's Mission* explains this saying,

> They (Adam and Eve) were to reflect God's kingship by being his vice-regents on earth. Because Adam and Eve were to subdue and rule 'over all the earth, it is plausible to suggest that they were to extend the geographic boundaries of the garden until Eden covered the whole earth... They were to extend the smaller livable area of the garden by transforming the outer chaotic region into a habitable territory.[21]

The end goal of the mission was for the entire earth to be filled with the knowledge of the glory of Lord. This concept is picked up by prophets when they say such things as:

---

[21] G.K. Beale, *The Temple and the Church's Mission: A Biblical Theology of Dwelling place of God* (Downers Grove: Il, InterVarsity Press,2004, 82.

"For the earth shall be filled with the knowledge of the glory of the LORD, as the waters cover the sea." – Habakkuk 2:14

"For the earth will be filled with the knowledge of the LORD as the waters cover the sea" – Isaiah 11:9

"The LORD will be king over the whole earth. On that day there will be one LORD, and his name the only name." – Zechariah 14:9

If Adam and Eve were faithful, they would have taken their perfect relationship which they had with each other and with the Lord and taken that to the ends of the earth. Beale once again is helpful in explaining this when he says, "God's ultimate goal in creation was to magnify His glory throughout the earth by means of His faithful image-bearers inhabiting the world in obedience to the divine mandate."[22] Adam and Eve's relationship, which reflected a greater relationship that existed with God, was intended to continue on with their children and their children's children. The end result would worshipers filling the earth with God's glory. Friendships were established with this mission in mind. The mission was not "Plan B" or something

---

[22] Ibid, 82.

that was deemed necessary after the fall of man. The fall only made the mission more difficult. Friendships are meant to be gasoline on the fire for God's global mission. When the serpent enters into the Garden that is when the problems in the mission start to occur.

"MISSION IMPOSSIBLE"

Just as sin caused Adam and Eve's relationship to go haywire, it also caused difficulty with their mission. In this story there was no Tom Cruise with a self-destructing tape or a Jack Bauer on the immediate horizon. The mission was now impossible. The mission also was not abandoned. It only became exceedingly more difficult. The curses that were placed upon Adam and Eve directly impacted the mission God gave them. Adam and Eve were called to be "fruitful and multiple", but women will now have difficulty in child-bearing (Gen 3:16). In Genesis 2:15, God gave man instruction for caring for the Garden, He told him to "work it and keep it." Remember the mission was to expand the Garden's boundaries until the Garden was the whole earth. Adam and Eve failed at keeping this task. As a result of this, God also places a judgment upon man saying,

> *"Cursed is the ground because of you; in pain you shall eat of it all the days of your*

life; thorns and thistles it shall bring forth for you; and you shall eat the plants of the field. By the sweat of your face you shall eat bread, till you return to the ground." (Gen. 3:17-19)

Bruce Waltke recognizing this connection between the curse and the mission says, "The man's natural relationship to the ground—to rule over it—is reversed; instead of submitting to him, it resists and eventually swallows him."[23] Mankind was punished, but this did not absolve the mission. Adam and Eve were then kicked out of the Garden, similar to how Israel would be kicked out of the land (i.e., the New Garden) because of their sin. The next main character in the narrative is Noah. Noah after the flood is then given the same commission as Adam to "be fruitful and multiply and fill the earth."

Noah is given the task of taking on the mission. Noah likewise stumbles. Similar to the Garden there is shame as a result of nakedness. This time Noah is shamed because of his son Ham. Noah then places a curse upon Ham just as God placed a curse upon Adam and Eve. Once again the hope of the mission seems to be waning. After Noah the readers are told about the people of Babel. As mentioned previously rather than establishing a city that makes much of the

---

[23] Waltke, 95.

Lord, they sought to make much of their own name and get glory for themselves. The next key figure to pickup the baton is a man named Abram.

Abram similar to Noah offers hope that the mission will be accomplished. Jason Meyer demonstrates this hope by saying,

> In contrast to the five uses of 'curse' up to this point Genesis 1-11, Genesis 12:2-3 uses the word 'bless' five times as a reversal of the curse. Through Abram, all the families of the earth shall be blessed (12:3). In contrast to the conduct of the citizens of Genesis 11 (they tried to make a name for themselves), God himself is going to make Abram's name great.[24]

The contrast between Babel and Abram gives the reader the first gleam of hope. Up to this point there has a trend of God giving a command, which is then followed by man's failure to keep that command. With Abram the reader experiences something new. No longer does the reader hear curse, curse, but now he gets to hear about the Lord's plan to bless the world through this man. The people of Babel sought to make a

---

[24] Jason C. Meyer, *Preaching: A Biblical* Theology (Wheaton: Il, Crossway Publishing Company, 2013), 86.

great name for themselves. In contrast to these people the reader gets to see how God is going to make this man's name great. Through Abram we see a transition, one which is not divorced from God's mission. Through Abram the mission of God would be accomplished. Sydney Greidanus once again is helpful with connecting Abram back to the fulfillment of the original mission when he says,

> *As to the context, God's promise to Abraham in Genesis 17:6, 'I will make you exceedingly fruitful' (c. V 2), harks back to the creation story, 'be fruitful and multiple' (Gen 1:28), as well as God's covenant with Noah, "Be fruitful and multiple' (Gen 9:1,7). Abram is another Adam, another Noah, with whom God makes a new beginning to establish his kingdom on earth.*[25]

The mission once again comes to the forefront through Abram. Abram later changed to Abraham, fails to accomplish the mission. Abraham fails to protect the promised seed when he goes down to Egypt and has Sarah lie that she is his husband. Abraham does this once again with Abimelech in Genesis 20. Abraham and Sarah attempt to expedite the promised seed of

---

[25] Greidanus, 159.

God, rather than waiting on God's timing through their servant Hagar. Even though Abraham fails to accomplish the mission, the Lord does not go back on His promises. Sin and the serpent once again accomplish their goal and seem to frustrate the mission. Sin has the same affect in our relationships by hindering us from accomplishing God's mission.

The way in which sin works in our friendships is by removing any thought of the mission from it. Brad House discussing community accurately recognizes the problem when he says, "Mission is generally the most neglected aspect of community within the church today." [26] What is true of community is certainly true with friendships as well. Satan does not mind for people to be friends. The thing in which sin and Satan strive to prevent is friendship that is focused on mission. No harm, no foul when people spend time together. The problem occurs when friends use their relationship to engage the world for Christ. One tangible way in which sin works to prevent mission in our relationships is by creating a desire to only befriend people who are like us. Let me give you an example.

When I first went to Bible College I met a guy who was completely different than I was. When I first saw him I would have to confess that I was

---

[26] Brad House, *Community: Taking Your Small Group off Life Support* (Wheaton:IL, Crossway Publishing Company, 2011),105.

judgmental. The thing that stood out about him was his all his tattoos and gauged earrings. I am from a southern suburban town and had not encountered many people like this. God in His providence slowly started putting us around each other. It seemed like every class that I had, he wound up being in also. I slowly began to converse with him. This guy has become an incredible friend. He later participated in my wedding. I cannot tell you where I would be spiritually without this particular friendship. This friend has caused me to think through numerous issues that I would've never thought through if I had not thrown out my sinful prejudices. This is how sin works. Sin hinders mission in our relationships by causing us to only befriend those who are most like us. As a result of this, we rob ourselves of so many things we could learn and experience from others. Paul first evangelized Philippi. Afterwards, Philippi ends up being a blessing to Paul and his ministry. Paul likewise evangelizes Ephesus. By the end of his ministry there he has been deeply impacted by the relationships he developed there. When Paul leaves Ephesus it is followed by everyone weeping. Sin seeks to prevent these types of friendships from coming about. Sin is working to prevent God's mission from being accomplished. Is there hope that the mission will be accomplished? Is there an unforeseen move that will result in a future checkmate?

MISSION ACCOMPLISHED

William Carey was born in the town Paulerspury in Northampton, England on August 17 1761. Carey was born to a faithful Church of England family. Through the reading of scripture and Jonathan Edward's Life and Dairy of David Brainerd Carey developed a heart to reach the nations for the name of Christ. In 1792 Carey organized a missionary society whose sole purpose was to reach the unreached. In 1793 Carey set sail for India to reach one of these people groups that had never heard the gospel. At the end of Carey's ministry, he had translated the bible into 42 different languages that previously had no access to scripture. William Carey would later be given the nickname the Father of the Modern Missions Movement.

Carey was passionate about calling others to reach the unreached. Carey once stated, "Multitudes sit at ease and give themselves no concern about the far greater part of their fellow sinners, who to this day, are lost in ignorance and idolatry."[27] Carey exemplifies a man who did not lose track of God's mission. William Carey is widely known for his heart for missions, but what

---

[27]http://www.christianitytoday.com/ch/131christians/missionaries/carey.html

many people do not realize is how his great accomplishments would've been impossible without his closest friends. Michael Haykin explains the modern ignorance of this crucial aspect of Carey's ministry by saying, "What is not so well-known today is the utterly vital help he received from friends who shared his vision to the full." Haykin goes on to give detail on what this relationship looked saying,

> *Carey would not have achieved an inkling of what he did. In fact, when Carey went to India, Fuller later said it was as if Carey had found a rich gold mine. Carey himself was more than willing to descend into the mine, but would Fuller and his other friends hold the rope that lowered him down? Fuller and the others in England vowed to hold the rope until they quit this earthly scene. Whenever God has done a great work in the history of the church it has always been through a team of men and women.*[28]

Carey's missionary accomplishments would not have been possible without his friends holding the rope for him, so that he could be

---

[28] Michael Haykin, "A Dull Flint: Andrew Fuller— Rope-Holder, Critic of Hyper-Calvinism & Missionary Pioneer" pg. 1 cited from http://www.andrewfullercenter.org/files/andrew-fuller.pdf

lowered down into this gold mine. God's mission is not something that can be accomplished alone or in isolation. In light of this all, how then is God's mission accomplished?

The book of Matthew begins by speaking of the birth of a child. Matthew tells the readers that this child is the "son of Abraham." We have already seen how Abraham was given the task of taking of God's original mission for mankind. Abraham like those before him failed at keeping this task. Even though Abraham failed at this task God remained faithful to His word that he would accomplish the mission through Abraham's seed. God promised that through Abraham's seed the whole earth will be blessed. Sydney Greidanus is helpful in showing the progression of the promise of the seed up to this point, when he says,

> Through your offspring [seed] all the nations on earth will be blessed.' That seed was first of all Isaac, Jacob, and then Joseph... But ultimately the 'seed' was Jesus Christ, 'son of Abraham' (Matt 1:1) through whom all the nations would be blessed because he was 'the Lamb of God who takes away the sin of world' (John 1:29). [29]

---

[29] Greidanus, 212.

Matthew is tying together all that was said before him and showing how it has culminated in the birth of this child. Donald Hagner recognizing the connection between the promise to Abraham and the birth of Christ says, "The Abrahamic covenant (Gen 12:1-3) speaks of blessing through Abraham for 'all the families of the earth.' In Jesus, through the line of Abraham, that promise is fulfilled."[30] Matthew begins his book making a "declaration" about this child and then ends the book by demonstrating how that declaration was proven true.

Matthew ends his book with Jesus commissioning his closest friends to the nations to fulfill the mission. Jesus truly is the son of Abraham who has come to bless the nations and thus fulfill the mission of God. Not only does Jesus commission his disciples to the nations, but as mentioned in the previous chapter, he reminds them that he is with them always. The significance of this is that Jesus is filling the earth with the presence of God. It is through Christ that the previous mentioned promises from the prophets are fulfilled. Through Christ the earth will be filled with the knowledge of the glory of the Lord as the waters cover the sea. How then does Jesus' finished work on the cross impact the mission of our friendships?

---

[30] Donald, A Hagner, *Word Biblical Commentary vol. 33a* (Grand Rapids:Mi, Word Publishing Company, 1993), 8.

THE MISSION OF FRIENDSHIP

After Christ's resurrection the disciples were told to wait on the Spirit. The disciples were told once they receive Him they will be witnesses in "Jerusalem and in all Judea and Samaria, and to the end of the earth." Christ sent the disciples to finish the mission. Because of Christ's finished work, the completion of the mission is certain. The mission that was given to the disciples has been passed on to the church. Believers now act as vice-regents or agents carrying on this mission. The way in which the gospel transforms friendship is through restoring this key aspect to the center of our relationships.

This mission is not simply encouraging each other on to go to the nations. This mission involves spurring friends on to engage their coworkers, neighbors, families, and cultures. The gospel transformed friendship does not hide from culture. It does not say stay away you are bad. The gospel transformed friendship engages its culture seeking to reclaim it for the name of Christ. The author of Hebrews shows how one implication of a person's redemption is that he spurs others and encourages others on to good works. The author explains this when he says,

> *"Since we have a great priest over the house of God, let us draw near with a true heart in full assurance of faith, with our hearts sprinkled clean from an evil conscience and our bodies washed with pure water. Let us*

hold fast the confession of our hope without wavering, for he who promised is faithful. And let us consider how to stir up one another to love and good works, not neglecting to meet together, as is the habit of some, but encouraging one another, and all the more as you see the Day drawing near."

When the gospel takes root in a believer's life, it enlists him into the mission of God. The gospel transformed friendship makes his brother get off the couch and stop watching CSI and NCSI reruns and go out and make a difference in the world for the name of Christ. The gospel transformed friendship spurs on mission by helping other believers fight against sin.

What does holiness have to do with the mission of God? Everything! The mission of God has always been about taking what was true in the Garden and expanding it until it fills the entire earth. Adam and Eve were called to work and keep the Garden. If they were faithful to their calling they would have kicked the serpent out of the Garden. The Garden was where God dwelt. God cannot be in the presence of sin. Christians are the new temple, with Christ being the cornerstone. Christians are called to help other believers fight to bring holiness and purity in the lives of God's new humanity. Paul, in Galatians 6, demonstrates the responsibility that each believer has in the sanctification of others. Paul explains this by saying, "Brothers, if anyone is caught in any transgression, you who are spiritual should restore him in a spirit of gentleness." John Piper shows how our sanctification demands gospel centered friendship when he says, "Sanctification is a community project."[31] When a believer sins, he is acting like Adam when he listened to the serpent. The believer acts as if he knows better than the Lord. The gospel transformed friendship seeks to restore Christ's lordship over all of life. This type of friendship demands that we help one another fight sin. It is restoring the broken image of God back into the lives of his new humanity. Part of restoring the image of God in our lives is through understanding our new identity in Christ. In the next chapter we are going to examine how friendships help with our identity crisis.

---

[31] John Piper, "Brothers, Save the Saints" http://www.desiringgod.org/articles/brothers-save-the-saints

APPLICATION

1. Is mission a vital part of friendship? (DISCUSS)

2. How can you keep mission at the center of your friendships? (DISCUSS)

3. Plan an evangelistic event invite at your house (e.g., block party, a barbeque, etc). Both you and your friends invite your neighbors for the purpose of building relationships and sharing the gospel. (PLAN)

4. Start a bible study group in your local community. Meet someone public. Allow others to join. (PLAN)

5. Find a friend and devote yourself to praying for the lost and an unengaged people group around the world.

6. Read about Paul's time in Ephesus in Acts 19 and 20 (READ)

7. How can you use your friendships to help "hold the rope" so the missionaries from your church can "mine the gold"?

IDENTITY IN FRIENDSHIP

"You should not believe your conscience and your feelings more than the word which the Lord who receives sinners preaches to you."
– Martin Luther

"If then you have been raised with Christ, seek the things that are above, where Christ is, seated at the right hand of God. Set your minds on things that are above, not on things that are on earth. For you have died, and your life is hidden with Christ in God."
– Colossians 3:1-3

"Spiritual identity means we are not what we do or what people say about us. And we are not what we have. We are the beloved daughters and sons of God."
– Henri Nouwen

IDENTITY IN FRIENDSHIP

One of my favorite TV shows as a child was Saved by the Bell. The show took place in Bayside High. The cast varied throughout its generations but the core cast was consistent. The main cast consisted of: Zack Morris, A.C. Slator, Lisa Turtle, Screech, Jessie Spano, and Kelly Kapowski. One of the major themes throughout the entirety of the show was Zack and Kelly's relationship. Kelly was the very popular cheerleader. Zack was the cool kid on campus, who carried around an amazing enormous cell-phone and got into trouble all the time. Zack and Kelly's relationship status changed more than Brett Favre's decision to retire. By the time they hit the college years you start to wonder, "Are they ever going to get married?" The series concluded with what everyone waited for Zack and Kelly getting married in Las Vegas.

The length of this show spanned almost my entire childhood and into my teenage years.

I later found out that the actors, who played these characters, did not really get married. I thought to myself, how could this be? Zack and Kelly were meant to be together! I could not divorce their television personalities from their true identities. What I experienced with these actors was a misguided or misplaced identity. The struggle was not who they were, but who I thought they were or should be. Christians often have this same type of misguided or misplaced identity in their own lives. We forget that our new identity is in Christ. Christians are so used to living their old life, they forget that they have been created new in Christ. As a result of this, Christians constantly fall back into their old lifestyle patterns and thus never live life as if they are part of the new humanity. A friend who has been transformed by the gospel is called to help his friends remember who they are in Christ. In order to understand who we are we need to understand who we were created to be and what caused our identity crisis.

IDENTITY ESTABLISHED & BROKEN

When man was created his identity was tied up in his relation to God. God was Adam and Eve's God and they were His people. Man's identity was never intended to be divorced from his relationship with God. Throughout the Old Testament the people of Israel are described as "God's people" (e.g., Genesis 26:24, 31:42, 32:9, Exodus 3:6, 9:1,etc.). The identity of the people of

Israel was tied up in their relationship with the Lord. Just as I could not disassociate the actor from the character, so the people of Israel could not be disassociated from their creator and Lord. All of humanity was created with this identity. It is not until sin enters into the picture that there arises confusion and loss of man's created identity.

Once the fall of man occurs there arises a tension between the seed of the serpent (cf., Genesis 3, Revelation 20:2) and the seed of promise (Genesis 3:15). No longer is all of humanity tied to their intended identity. There are now two separate identities. The first example of this could be seen with Cain. As mentioned earlier, Jesus ties Cain to Satan when he calls Satan "a murderer from the beginning." When Pharaoh and his army cross the Red Sea and are crushed by the water, they are later compared to Leviathan the serpent. At the crossing of the Red Sea, God crushed the head of Leviathan (cf., Psalm 74:13-14, Isaiah 27:1). Once again the people who are against God and His promises are identified with the serpent. A New Testament example of this identity association is when Jesus calls the Pharisees a "Brood of Vipers." A "Brood of Vipers" is a seed of a serpent.[32] People are tied to their identity. There are many examples throughout scripture of people who do not live like the people they are

---

[32] I owe this connection to Dr. Jim Hamilton.

called to be. In some situations it is a bad thing (e.g., God's people Israel begin living like godless people). In other situations it can result in a person finding the Lord's favor. One great example of this is with the story of Rachel and Leah.

Leah was a girl that was very much tied to her identity. The first thing that is said about Leah is that her "eyes were weak." There is some uncertainty as to what this means exactly. Scholars agree though that it is a sign of her unattractiveness. Tim Keller explains the writer's use of the term "weakness" and its association to Leah's looks by saying, "Weakness probably means cross-eyed; it could mean something unsightly. But here is the point: Leah was particularly unattractive, and she had to live all of her life in the shadow of her sister who was absolutely stunning."[33] Leah is described in contrast to her sister Rachel. Rachel is described as "beautiful in form and appearance." Leah undoubtedly lived a life in the shadow of her beautiful sister.

The story of Rachel and Leah begins with Jacob meeting Rachel at a well. This is definitely reminiscent of the beginnings of his father Isaac and Rebecca's relationship at a well. Jacob begins

---

[33] Timothy Keller, "The Girl that Nobody Wanted" in *Heralds of the King: Christ-Centered Sermons in the Tradition of Edmund P. Clowney* ed. Dennis Johnson (Wheaton:Il, Crossway Publishing Company, 2009), 63.

working for Laban, the father of Rachel and Leah. Laban asks Jacob, "What do you want for pay for your labor?" Jacob responds by saying that he wants "the beautiful Rachel." Jacob agrees to work for seven years in order to get his prize of Rachel. At the end of the seven years a party is thrown and Jacob is supposed to receive his bride.

The party likely included drinking, a heavily veiled bride, and a dark tent due to the lack of electricity. Jacob went into the tent and Leah, not Rachel went into the tent with him. In the morning Jacob woke up to realize that he had not married Rachel, but that he had married the unattractive Leah. Jacob naturally is enraged by this transaction. Laban then offers to give Rachel to Jacob if he agrees to serve him another seven years. Jacob agrees to this new transaction. You may wonder why Jacob would agree to the additional requirements. There are two things going on here. First, we are able to see Jacob's deep love for Rachel. Second, there seems to be a connection between Laban response to Jacob and Jacob's previous deception of his father Isaac. Laban acts as a wordsmith with his pointed jab/ response to Jacob. Robert Alter explains this well by saying,

> *Laban is an instrument of dramatic irony: his perfectly natural reference to 'our place' has the effect of touching a nerve of guilty*

conscience in Jacob, who in his place acted to put the younger before the firstborn...the deceiver deceived, deprived by darkness of the sense of sight as his father is by blindness, relying, like his father, on the misleading sense of touch.[34]

Jacob asks, why did you deceive me? Laban responds by connecting his deception to Jacob's deception of his father Isaac. Jacob then serves the additional seven years and also marries Rachel. After Jacob marries Rachel, Leah once again returns to the shadow of her sister. Leah has now become the unattractive and unloved wife. Leah then begins to think that she can gain the attention of her husband by having children with him. The writer describes this by saying,

"When the Lord saw that Leah was hated, he opened her womb, but Rachel was barren. And Leah conceived and bore a son, and she called his name Reuben, for she said,'Because the Lord has looked upon my affliction; for now my husband will love me.' She conceived again and bore a son, and said, 'Because the Lord has heard that I am

---

[34] Robert Alter, *Genesis: Commentary and Translation* (New York: New York, W.W. Norton and Company, 1997), 155.

hated, he has given me this son also.' And she called his name Simeon. Again she conceived and bore a son, and said, 'Now this time my husband will be attached to me, because I have borne him three sons. (Genesis 29:31-34)'"

Rather than finding her identity in the Lord, Leah starts to find her identity both in her husband and through having children. Once Leah realized that she was not gaining her husband's eye through having children she finally makes a change. A transition occurs with the birth of Leah's fourth child. With the birth of the fourth child the writer tells us "And she conceived again and bore a son, and [Leah] said, 'This time I will praise the Lord.' Therefore she called his name Judah." No longer will she find her identity through children and her husband. With this child, Leah will now serve the Lord. No longer will her identity be caught up in trying to gain the attention of her husband. Keller once again is helpful in recognizing her transition when he says, "At that point, she has finally taken her heart's deepest hopes off of the old way, off of her husband and her children, and she has put them in the Lord."[35] Leah has returned to her true identity, the one which tells her that her value is more than her looks, her children, or how much

---

[35] Keller, 68.

she is loved by others. Leah's identity has returned to its rightful state of being bound up in her relation to the Lord.

It is nearly impossible to not turn on the television and hear a story as someone self-identifying as another gender, race, or etc. We live in a culture that teaches you that you can be whatever you want to be, but being who you are is never enough. When you come to the story of Jacob, Rachel, and Leah, we may be quick to jump the the conclusion that Leah and her response to how Jacob treated her was crazy. Leah begins naming her children with hopes of gaining the attention of Jacob. If we were honest we are more like Leah than we want to admit. We long for the attention of others. We work for identity in our friendships. How often do you see people who have changed everything about themselves just to fit into a certain crowd? Rather than friends enjoying diversity and the unique aspects of who are you, you feel like you have to change who you are in order to be who you think they want you to be. In our friendships we often work incredibly hard to hide who we really are from our friends. We create false identities in hopes that our friends will like us more. You may think you are not attractive or fit enough, so you strive to change your appearance in hopes that you will be better accepted. Living a healthy lifestyle is not wrong, but your motivation should never be to make others care more about you. The series Authentic Manhood is spot on when it says, "Men are taught to work for identity and not from identity." What it says about men applies to all of humanity. Society tells you that you need to work for your identity. Society tells you that if you are going to be something that you must move up the corporate ladder, have the nice things, and know the right people. "In competitive sports this is true as well. An athlete is only as good as his last pass, catch, or shot. Instead of working from a place of shalom (i.e., peace which comes from God) and peace in your heart, which God gives you, you work to attain that peace and you can never rest because you never are quite good enough. So winning becomes everything and losing is devastating." Scripture tells a different story. "When you have the shalom of God already in your heart you can take both winning and losing in stride." Scripture tells you that you are greater than what you own, how you look, and where you work. The story of Rachel and Leah does not end with Leah in disparity, without hope, or an identity.

IDENTITY RESTORED

Leah has several children with Jacob. One of those children was named Judah. It is through Judah that Jesus the messiah would come. In John 4 Jesus arrives at a setting, quite similar to the one where Isaac met Rebecca, quite similar to the one where Jacob met Rachel. Jesus arrives at a well. We are told that this well is no ordinary well, but it is known as the "well of Jacob." Here at the well Jesus meets a woman similar to Leah. This woman is both spiritually unattractive and unloved. This particular woman has had several husbands and the man that she was living with was not even her husband. This woman has gathered at Jacob's well to receive water that would briefly sustain her for her daily labor. Water from the well of Jacob may sustain her momentarily, but the water from the man that she met at the well on this particular day would make it so that she will never thirst again. Jesus and this woman begin to converse. The woman spoke to Jesus saying, "I know that Messiah is coming (he who is called Christ). When he comes, he will tell us all things." Jesus said to her, "I who speak to you am he." Jacob served fourteen years to receive his beautiful wife Rachel. Jesus gives his entire life for this unattractive and unloved woman. This unloved woman received a new identity from Jesus. After receiving a new identity this woman goes out and shares the good news of everything she had heard from this man. As a result of her ministry we are told, "Many Samaritans from that town believed in him because of the woman's testimony (John 4:39a). All people are like this spiritually unattractive woman until Christ gives them a new identity. A new problem arises once we receive our identity. Christians often forget that they have been made new creations. Christians experience a sort of spiritual amnesia. Christians start forgetting who they are and what they have been saved from and to. Because of this spiritual amnesia a vital component of a Christian friendship is reminding each other who they are in Christ.

Spiritual disciplines are a vital part of the Christian life. Sometimes we wrongly view these vital aspects of the Christian life as the ultimate thing. We start to think God is not happy with me because I missed my quiet time this morning or God is not happy with me because I overslept and did not spend enough time in prayer. We slowly start to think that our standing with the Lord is based upon our daily performance. The Christian's right-standing with the Lord is based upon Christ's righteousness. The Christian never moves past this point. Gerhard Forde is helpful in explaining how all of the Christian life is tied back to a person's righteousness in Christ. Forde says that sanctification [i.e., everything after the moment that a person is justified] is "simply the art of getting used to justification." What Forde means by this is that, the Christian life is about learning to live in light of our new identity.

If you have ever visited another country, you know that there is a period of time where you have to adjust to the new culture. Some cultures have different eating habits, dress attire, shopping style, food options, and etc. When a person visits a new country he has to learn how to live in his new environment. Likewise, the

Christian will spend his entire life learning what it means to be a member of a different kingdom while living here on earth. The Christian learns to live life as a part of a new humanity. We were like the woman at the well, spiritually unattractive and deserving nothing. Christ came and gave us a new identity. Christ came and made beautify what was formerly unattractive and unloved. Our beauty is now bound up in Christ and his righteousness. We now live on the other side of the cross. We are like a person visiting a foreign country. We are learning "to get used our justification." This learning process is not something that can be done alone. A person that has been transformed by the gospel is called to help his brothers learn to live life in their new identity.

This type of friendship involves regularly helping others find their value and worth not in things of this world, but in their identity with the Lord. This sort of friendship reminds his conscience laden brother that Christ is bigger than how he feels about himself. Christian friendship involves helping his brother fight spiritual amnesia. This person reminds his fellow brothers and sisters of their new identity and what they have been saved from and saved to. Those who find their identity in the Lord are revitalized and strengthened by God's word. We will examine in the next chapter how scripture must be at the center Gospel Transformed Friendship.

APPLICATION

1. How can our friendships influence our identities both good and bad? (DISCUSS)

2. What are some places that people find their identity? (Discuss)

3. How can you fight "Spiritual Amnesia?" (DISCUSS)

4. Colossians 3:1-17 (READ)

5. Genesis 29 (READ)

6. Call a struggling friend and remind them that their worth is not in what they own, their looks, or what others think about them, but it is bound up in their redeemer (PLAN)

"Rather, speaking the truth in love, we are to grow up in every way into him who is the head, into Christ"
– Ephesians 4:15

"No Spiritual Discipline is more important than the intake of God's Word. Nothing can substitute for it. There simply is no healthy Christian life apart from a diet of the milk and meat of Scripture."
– Don Whitney

"We owe to the scriptures the same reverence as we owe to God, since it has its only source in Him and has nothing of human origin mixed with it."
– John Calvin

GOD'S WORD IN FRIENDSHIP

Words have a unique ability to inspire, buildup, and even tear down. One place you can see the power words have in the lives of others is at a sporting event. Fans chant things like brick and swing in hopes of altering the opposing player's game. Coaches also utilize words for the purpose of motivation. Coaches bring in special guests to the games for the sole purpose of motivating their players either before the game or at the halftime break. One of the best at this type of motivation is Ray Lewis. Ray Lewis is a former middle linebacker and captain for the Baltimore Ravens.

One of Ray Lewis's most notable motivational speeches took place when he was brought in as a special guest to speak to the Stanford Cardinal Basketball team during the NIT tournament. It had been over ten years since the Cardinals had won the NIT. The Cardinals had just lost in the second round of the Pac 10 conference championship to California. Afterwards, the Cardinals slowly made their way through the NIT tournament. Ray Lewis was invited to speak to the team before their game against the University of Massachusetts in the semi-finals of the tournament. Lewis said many things to the players that particular day which undoubtedly built excitement. Lewis encouraged the players saying, "Wins and losses come a dime a dozen, but effort? Nobody can judge effort. Because effort is between you and you."[36] Lewis's speech paid off. The Cardinals played above their game on this particular day and ended up winning the game. The Cardinals went on to win the entire tournament that particular year. Words play an important role in our everyday lives and friendships as well.

Have you ever had a friend who called you and said the right thing at the right time? Maybe he called just to give you an encouraging word. It could've been a call just to give you a word of hope during a difficult season of life. Friends have a unique ability to speak right to a person's heart. I can recount several situations where a dear friend either called or a visited and said the right thing at the right time. It was those words

---

[36] http://sports.yahoo.com/blogs/ncaab-the-dagger-college-basketball-blog/ray-lewis-delivers-stanford-pregame-locker-room-speech-010250239.html

that helped me get to the other side of a difficult trial in life. Not all words are positive in nature. Those who are the closest to you, ironically can be the ones who say the most hurtful words to you. Words both build up and tear down. Not only do words play a central role in our lives, they also do so throughout the narrative of scripture.

THE WORD ESTABLISHED & WORD FALLEN

At the very beginning of the book of Genesis words take the center-stage. Scripture begins with God speaking creation into being. God spoke and created the light. God then spoke and created the waters. By God's word the waters were divided from the heavens and from the land. God spoke animals into being. God final creative act is speaking human beings into existence. God's words did not cease their creative power with the completion of creation. God's words continued their creative power through the rest of scripture.

In Matthew 8 a great storm takes place and Jesus is asleep on the boat. The sailors became afraid for their lives because of the storm. The sailors woke Jesus up and asked him to save them from this storm. Jesus spoke to the storm and it obeyed his voice. Just as the waters obeyed God's voice at creation and separated the land and heavens, so they still obey his voice when he tells the storm to be still. Not only do God's words still hold power over the creation itself, but they still have the ability to create new life.

Jesus speaks to the four day dead Lazarus and creates life in him in John 11:43. Likewise, Jesus speaks and creates life in Jairus's dead daughter in Luke 8:54. As we have already seen in the book of James, God still creates through His word today. James demonstrates the word's life giving power when he says, "Of his own will he brought us forth by the word of truth, that we should be a kind of first fruits of his creatures." Salvation and God's word are tied together. God's word both creates and sustains life.

God's word sustains the life which it created. Job after experiencing many hardships in his life said "I have not departed from the command of His lips; I have treasured the words of His mouth more than my necessary food (Job 23:12)." How is it that a person lives life through great tragedies? It is through clinging to the word of God. Job models how God's word sustains life even in the midst of tragedy. Not only does it give the ability to preserve through tragedy, but it also gives strength in a person's normal everyday life. The Psalmist compares the person who meditates upon God's word daily to that of a strong tree that yields fruit in season and out of season which does not wither.[37] God's word both creates and sustains every part of life. From the garden to the grave, God's word has and will always create and sustain. Friendship was created by God's word and it was meant to be sustained by it. The way in which sin uses its destructive powers to ruin friendships is by removing God's word from its rightful place.

God's word was meant to be at the center of all relationships. It was meant to create and sustain new friendships. Its frequency was to be regular and normative. When sin enters into the picture it is like the relationships took a blindsided tackle from Ray Lewis. Once relationships dusted themselves off and got off the ground, the hope of recovery seemed distant if not impossible.

After God created Adam and Eve He placed them in the Garden. The Garden was supposed to be a place where both God and His word were its center. The first thing that the serpent does in the Garden is to call into question God's word (Genesis 3:4). The serpent causes man to question both the word of God and the character of God. Is God's word truthful? Can you really take God at His word? The dilemma ends with Adam and Eve believing the serpent rather than the Lord. Once

---

[37] One who meditates daily upon the word of God is described in Edenic language. The Aramaic meaning of this word is 'fruitful' or 'well-watered'." It is as if he has returned to enjoying the presence of the Lord in the Garden.

sin enters into the world man no longer enjoyed the fellowship that was originally present. God's word was no longer at the center of his people. God's word went from being the norm in the life of His to being something that was distant or far away from them. Rachel and Leah provide a valuable lesson about identity and it will be through their son Joseph that the hope of God's word returning to its rightful place in will occur.

Joseph was one of the last children of Jacob. Jacob loved Joseph more than he did any of his other children. Because of the love his father had for him, animosity continually grew between him and his brothers. During this time God's word was distant from His people. The Lord began to reveal the future to Joseph through dreams. Joseph's dreams made his brothers only hate him the more. The animosity toward Joseph continued to grow until it reached its breaking point. Joseph's brothers plotted to kill him. Joseph's brothers threw him into a pit and left him to die. A short time later Joseph's brothers see a crowd of people coming and think, rather than leaving him to die for nothing, they can actually sell him and make a profit. Joseph's brothers then raise him out of the pit and go and sell him for a bag of silver. Joseph was then sold again. This time he wound up serving Potiphar, one of Pharaoh's officers.

God's hand was upon Joseph the entire time he served Potiphar. One day, Potiphar's wife tried to coerce Joseph into lying with her. Joseph refused and ran from her. Potiphar's wife then lied and said that Joseph tried to rape her and she screamed. After she screamed, she claimed that Joseph fled. Potiphar was naturally enraged by this. Potiphar throws Joseph into prison for this crime. The Lord's hand continued to be on Joseph even while he was in prison.

While Joseph was in prison two men had dreams. Joseph approached the men and said, "Do not interpretations belong to God? Tell it to me, please." Joseph's statements testify to two realities. First, Joseph acknowledged that only the Lord knows all things. Second, Joseph's confession points out that God's word alone brings clarity to the hidden things. After Adam and Eve were kicked out of the Garden, God's word began coming through vision, dreams, and his prophets. Samuel picks up this idea when he says, "'Why have you disturbed me by bringing me up?' And Saul answered, 'I am greatly distressed; for the Philistines are waging war against me, and God has departed from me and no longer answers me, either through prophets or by dreams' (1 Sam 28:15)." Saul, like Joseph, recognized that only God's revelation could bring clarity.

God's word alone reveals to the hidden things. Adam and Eve once enjoyed this without restraint, but now sin has made it so that God's word is distant and hidden. God's word will not remain hidden from His people. In the story of Joseph, God gives the meaning to the dreams to

Joseph to reveal to his fellow prisoners. A few years after this took place Pharaoh had a dream that needed interpreting as well. A word came to Pharaoh that someone he had in prison had the ability to interpret dreams, one who could reveal the hidden things of the Lord. Pharaoh then calls on Joseph with hopes that he could interpret his dream. The Lord reveals the meaning of the dream to Pharaoh through Joseph. Because of Joseph's interpretation Pharaoh clothes Joseph in fine linen and placed him in authority over all of Egypt. Even though the story of Joseph ends with a gleam of hope, God's word still had not returned to the center of His people.

GOD'S WORD RESTORED

From where would the hope of this restoration come? The story of Jesus is very similar to that of Joseph. Jesus was betrayed by those who were closest to him. Jesus much like Joseph was sold for silver. Just as Joseph was cast into a pit to die by those closest to him, Jesus was put to death by his own people. After being cast into a pit to die, Joseph was raised to new life where he was given authority over all of Egypt. Jesus after his death was raised to new life and given authority over the heavens and earth. The Lord revealed to Joseph the hidden meanings of both Pharaoh and the prisoner's visions. Jesus was the greater Joseph; he is God's word made flesh. It is through Jesus that the word of God will return to the center of his people's lives.

The Gospel of John begins by saying that "in the beginning was the word and that the word was with God and the word was God. He was in the beginning with God. All things came into being though Him, and apart from Him nothing came into being that has come into being." John explains that God's word created the universe. John depicts the word as a person. Who is this word that was with God and was God? John answers this question by saying that the "word" became "flesh" and dwelt among us. John was referring to Jesus. It is through Jesus that God's "word" returns to His people. The writer of Hebrews reiterates this when he says, "Long ago, at many times and in many ways, God spoke to our fathers by the prophets, but in these last days he has spoken to us by his Son, whom he appointed the heir of all things, through whom also he created the world." What Joseph came and provided hope for Jesus made a reality. We find hope in our friendships by bringing the word by to its rightful place through Jesus Christ. What creates and sustains a friendship? The thing that creates and sustains a friendship is very thing that has been creating and sustaining since the creation of the universe: the word of God.

It seems like any time there is a difficult decision to make in life, man naturally turns into a mystic. Everything during this time becomes a sign. This mysticism starts at an early age. Little girls pick pedals off of daisies in hopes that the last pedal will give surety of a relationship with their potential beau. More often than not this is played for fun, but the mystical idea which this game promotes only grows as people mature. One of the clearest places to see this is when a person is trying to determine whether the girl/guy they are dating is "the one." I have always wondered what it would be like being a mystic and living in area like Las Vegas or other wedding chapel areas. It seems everything would be a sign, pointing to what possibly could be the wrong decision. People are constantly looking to find the will of the Lord in their lives, but they look in all the wrong places. What role does the Gospel Transformed Friendship play in helping make the difficult decisions in life? The Gospel Transformed Friendship brings scripture back to its rightful place in a person's life.

God's word was always supposed to be at the center of our relationships. It was not until sin entered into the world that God's word was misplaced. The Gospel Transformed Friendship brings that word back to the center of our lives and relationships. When a difficult decision in life comes around Gospel Transformed friends are called to help their friends think through the lens of scripture.

All of scripture points and testifies to Christ. This demands us to bring your friends to the cross whenever difficult decisions in life take place. Friends are there to help you answer the question, "In what ways will my decision best magnify Christ?" This looks like helping your friends flee from mysticism and clinging to God's word. Propaganda, a Christian hip hop artist, provides a helpful analogy of this type of tendency saying, "It's boring when my life is more like the book of Ruth than Exodus"[38] Everyone wants to have a burning bush or a parting of the seas experience when it comes to difficult decisions. We want God to verbally tell us what to do. Our decision process really looks more like a Ruth situation, where God puts the right person or friend in our life at the right time. When you are trying to determine whether to take a job, propose to a potential suitor, or etc. godly friends are an essential part of the process. The author of Proverbs demonstrates our need for others during the decision-making process of life when he says such things as:

> *"Where there is no guidance, a people falls, but in an abundance of counselors there is safety." – Proverbs 11:14*

---

[38] Propaganda, quoted from Beautiful Eulogy's Instruments of Mercy "Signs and Symbols" (Humble Beast Records, 2013).

"The way of a fool is right in his own eyes, but a wise man listens to advice." – Proverbs 12:15

"Without counsel plans fail, but with many advisers they succeed." – Proverbs 15:22

Once a person has been transformed by the gospel he realizes that he no longer needs the casting of lots to determine the will of the Lord. Christians have been given the Holy Spirit, who has drawn them together, who convicts and leads them together towards righteous living. Christians, now through the Spirit, speak God's word into each other's lives and challenge them to think biblically when it comes to life decisions. I remember how liberating this was for me when I realized that I wasn't called to find the hidden will of the Lord. This liberation also comes with a responsibility to others. Although I am liberated to this freedom, I am also obligated then to others. A good place to see both of these aspects is in 1 Timothy 3.

When a person is considering being a pastor, he should first examine his desires. Here we see one aspect of the decision making process. A person should ask, "For what has God given me a desire?" A person's desires play an important part in the decision-making process. God changes or can desire the desires of a person's heart. Desire is not sufficient to make the final decision.

Sometimes our desires can be deceptive. This is where the Gospel Transformed Friendship is counter-cultural. Culture says that our desires are ultimate. "Whatever you want, keep working at until you accomplish it." Culture also tells you that anyone who gets in the way of your desires is simply a speed bump in the road toward your ultimate destination. Paul tells Timothy in 1 Timothy that desire is not sufficient, but that we need others to examine our lives to determine whether our desires match the calling. I once had someone tell me that God was calling them to international missions. This particular person had been clean off of drugs for about a week and he was not a member of a church. Our culture would tell this man, praise the Lord and go for it. The Gospel Transformed friendship would call into question this person's desires, call him to repent and join a church. Along these same lines, Paul tells Timothy that not only must a person have the desires but the church must also confirm that qualities within this person's life. A gospel transformed friendship gives scriptural counsel even when it calls into question a friend's desire. In the realm of pastoral calling, scripture calls for a man to examine his desires and then have others examine his life. There is freedom in that you do not have to find out the hidden mysteries of the Lord, because you have been given God's word and the church. Not only do gospel transformed friendships bring scripture to the forefront in the decision making process, but they also use scripture to build up the body of Christ.

Scripture is filled with passages calling other believers to meditate upon the word. Christians are called to store the word of God into their hearts that they may not sin against the Lord (Psalm 119:11). Christians are also called devote themselves to the public reading of scripture and to immerse themselves in the scriptures (1 Timothy 4:13-15). One of the most quoted passages on the subject of "scripture" is 2 Timothy 3:16-17. In this passage Paul says, "All Scripture is breathed out by God and profitable for teaching, for reproof, for correction, and for training in righteousness, that the man of God may be competent, equipped for every good work." All of the things which Paul mentions demand others to use scripture in our lives as a skilled surgeon uses a scalpel. Gospel Transformed Friends do not use scripture to beat a person up or tear him/her down. Gospel Transformed Friends use scripture to help remove the hidden cancer that is secretly killing the person. It removes the very thing that is keeping you away from looking more like Christ. These types of friendships help a person lay aside weights that slow him down, and remove sin which he clings so closely toward (Hebrews 12:1-2).These type of friendships use scripture to encourage and build one another up as Paul calls for in 1 Thessalonians 5:11 and Ephesians 4:29. I can pinpoint two particular times in my life, which were undoubtedly the most difficult times in my life. During both of these times I can also point to several different friends who were there and built me up by sharing God's word with me. Why is it then that we need scripture in our lives during these times? It is because God's word continues to do the work that has done since creation. God's word creates and sustains life. When you want to provide hope to the brother who has experienced a great tragedy, you go to God's word which sustains. When you have a friend who is wondering whether his family member will ever turn to the Lord, you then turn with them to God's word which creates life. Not only should you point them to the word's which create life, you should pray with them to the God who changes hearts. In the next chapter we will examine what role prayer plays in the Gospel Transformed Friendship.

APPLICATION

1. What role do words play in our relationships? (DISCUSS)

2. How does Christ come and restore God's word back to its rightful location? (DISCUSS)

3. (READ), James 1:19, Proverbs 11:14; 12:15, 15:22, Ephesians 4:29 2 Timothy 3:16

4. Look for ways to bring scripture into your relationships. (PLAN)

5. Call or text an encouraging or challenging word to a friend. (PLAN)

6. Apologize to a brother or sister for hurtful words which you may have said to them in the past or even recently. (PLAN)

"The first and last stages of holy living are crowned with praying"
– E.M. Bounds

""It is God's will through His wonderful grace, that the prayers of His saints should be one of the great principal means of carrying on the designs of Christ's kingdom in the world. When God has something very great to accomplish for His church, it is His will that there should precede it the extraordinary prayers of His people."
– Jonathan Edwards

""Prayer secret, fervent, believing prayer lies at the root of all personal godliness."
– William Carey

"Rejoice always, pray without ceasing, give thanks in all circumstances; for this is the will of God in Christ Jesus for you."
– 1 Thessalonians 5:16-18

PRAYER IN THE GARDEN TEMPLE

I have a six year old and a five year old. One thing about parenthood that I would have never predicted would be how much knowledge I would gain about cartoon and children's book characters. I cannot tell you how many times I have found myself driving down the road singing the Doc McStuffins' theme song. It is truly a terrible thing to get a children's cartoon song stuck in your head. I find it "to be" one of the most difficult things in life to get rid of. It is especially embarrassing when one of your friends asks you, "What you are humming?" There is really no appropriate response that could possibly redeem you. Parenting classes and parenting books do not prep you for the fact that you will slowly know more cartoon characters than you will real book and TV characters. My daughter would honestly think you were crazy if you told her that someone named Denzel Washington beat out Dora the Explorer for an Oscar on a given year. I remember the first time that my daughter saw a person dressed up as a cartoon character in real life. It was the first time that the cartoon world invaded her physical world.

My wife was out and I was in charge of taking care of the children for the day. I wanted to be the fun dad and I thought I would take my children to Chuck E. Cheese. I was excited to see my daughter's reaction when she saw the dressed up character for the first time. We arrive at Chuck E. Cheese and pick up our pizza. Right about the time we sat down at our table Chuck E. the Mouse comes out. I was not really prepared for the response which I received from this event. My daughter saw Chuck E. the Mouse and screamed and started crying. I found out that day that my daughter is terrified of people dressed up as animated characters. I later learned that she is not terrified of all characters, but only certain ones. About a year later my wife, daughter, and I had the joy of going to Disney on Ice and seeing all her favorite Disney characters skate and sing her favorite songs. On that occasion my daughter's two worlds invaded each other and it resulted in an unforgettable evening.

PRAYER ESTABLISHED & FALLEN

In the last chapter we discussed how in the Garden man was able to hear God's word freely. Once sin entered into the world God's word was displaced from its rightful position in our lives and relationships. In this chapter we will examine how not only did the Fall impact God's word to us, but it also impacted our ability to communicate with the Lord.

While Adam and Eve lived in the Garden "one world" existed. God dwelt in the presence of man. Man had the joy of living in God's space and in God's time. Before sin entered into the world, man could converse freely with the Lord. Sin entered into the world and man was kicked out of God's space and time. As a result of this, our communication with the Lord transformed dramatically. Where Adam and Eve could previously communicate as you and I could communicate with one another; this form of communication was now reserved only for a select few of God's people throughout the rest of the Old Testament. The primary way communication took place among God's people in the Old Testament was through prayer, but more specifically prayer at the temple (Luke 18:10; Acts 3:1;22:7). What was significant about this particular location?

Greg Beale is helpful in explaining the significance of this location when he says,

> *Indeed, Ezekiel 28 explicitly calls Eden the first sanctuary, which substantiates that Eden is described as a temple because it is*

the first temple, albeit a 'garden-temple'. Early Judaism confirms this identification. Indeed, it is probable that even the similar Ancient Near Eastern temples can trace their roots back to the original primeval garden.[39]

Beale elaborates on this even further when he says, "The Garden of Eden was the first archetypal temple, and that it was the model for all subsequent temples."[40] Once sin entered into the world, man could no longer dwell in the presence of the Lord. Man was then kicked out of the Garden, but the Lord did not leave them there alone. God desired to dwell among His people. The temple and the tabernacle were created so that man could once again dwell in the presence of the Lord. God was now in the midst of His people, but sacrifice was now needed in order for man to be in the presence of a perfectly holy God. When believers went to the temple to pray it was as if they were re-entering the Garden and were once again in the presence of the Lord. NT Wright demonstrates this connection when speaking about Psalm 141. Wright connects the prayer and the temple saying,

---

[39] Beale, 80.

[40] Ibid, 26.

Psalm 141, ... speaks of YHWH as a 'refuge' (141:8), sees personal and private prayer as the functional equivalent of being in the Temple—a necessity, of course, for the great majority of Jews even before the destruction of the Temple in AD 70, and for all of them thereafter.[41]

When a person prayed, but even more significantly prayed at the temple "two separate worlds" collided and made one unified world. Man could once again communicate with the Lord in His space and in his time. Prayer at the temple was as if man returned to the Garden and was once again able to walk and talk with the Lord. Even though man could once again return to God's space and time it did not mean that God would give His ear to all their requests. Sin was still present within the lives of his people. The sin issue needed to be addressed. Prior to the Fall, man's communication with God was trained by sin. After the Fall, we now have an issue of our prayers or our language to God being tainted. We pray, but our prayers are selfish and lack trust that the Lord will grant them (James 1:6-8). Paul says that we do not even know what to pray and

---

[41] N.T. Wright, *The Case for the Psalms: Why They are Essential* (New York: New York HarperOne Publishing Company, 2013), 99.

because of this the Spirit intercedes for us (Romans 8:26). Not only do our prayers lack trust and are selfish, we also do not know if we are praying for the right things.

I can remember several things that I earnestly prayed for as a child, that I look back on now and think, "Wow, I am glad the Lord did not grant that request." If the Lord had granted my request you would not be reading this right now because I would be living with my seven figure salary on the beach, sitting in a lawn chair, waiting on Commissioner Gordon to buzz me to the scene with the Bat-signal. Our prayers are confused and distorted because of sin. Not only are our personal prayers impacted by sin, but also our prayers for each other are impacted by sin.

I frequently have friends ask me to pray for them on a given issue that is going on in their lives. The difficult task is determining exactly how to pray for them. Do you pray that the Lord continues to mature this couple's relationship as they pursue hopes of marriage? Do you pray that a person gets a particular job that they have really been wanting or do you pray that they keep the one that they are already invested in and have relationships in? Prayer in friendships is often a difficult task. We pray the wrong things and we pray selfishly for our friends as well. We pray with our best interest in mind rather than the Lord's. I have always found it best to pray for the Lord to do whatever would bring Him the most glory. This sort of prayer demonstrates my inadequacies and lack of knowledge of God's will. It also demonstrates my trust in the fact that God does all things for the good of those in Christ. Sin has hindered even our communication with Lord. Is there hope that our communication with Lord will be rescued as well? To find that answer to that question, we will once again have turn to the New Testament.

PRAYER RESTORED

After cleansing the temple because the people were making the temple a house of trade, Jesus makes a remarkable statement. The Jews asked Jesus, "What sign do you show us for doing these things?" Jesus responds by saying, "Destroy this temple, and in three days I will raise it up." Those who were present did not understand Jesus' statements. The people's responses testified to their confusion as to what he meant. They respond to Jesus by saying, "It has taken forty-six years to build this temple, and you will raise it up in three days?" John then gives commentary to what seemed to be a confusing a statement. John explains that Jesus was referring to his body. Jesus is the greater temple of the Lord. The temple simply prepared God's people for the coming of Christ. Christ is the new greater temple. Where people formerly went to the temple to pray, Christians now pray to the Father through Christ. There is no longer a need for sacrifice in order for our prayers to be heard. Our prayers are now heard on the basis of Christ's perfect righteousness. John seeing a vision of the New Jerusalem points out that there is no temple (Revelation 21:22). Christ is now all. What does this mean for our prayers? Christians, just like God's people of the Old Testament, go to the temple to pray. The only difference is we now pray through the greater temple Jesus Christ. At this temple we don't need to bring a sacrifice because Christ is our sacrifice. Fred Sanders is helpful here in showing how we pray through Christ when he says,

> We are directed to pray to the Father in the name of Jesus, and it customary to do that by ending prayers with the formula 'in Jesus Name,' as an introduction to set up everything you are about to say. This calls attention to the fact that all Christian prayer is offered under this sign: 'Not by my authority or according to my fitness or deserving of a hearing, but on the basis of the finished work of Jesus Christ I approach God.'[42]

---

[42] Fred Sanders, *The Deep Things of God: How the Trinity Changes Everything* (Wheaton:Il, Crossway Publishing Company, 2010), 213.

PRAYER IN THE GARDEN TEMPLE

It is because of what Christ has done on our behalf that we are able to approach God. Christ is the spotless lamb, which makes it so we can once again enter into the fellowship which once existed in the Garden. The Christian prayer is a prayer that is through Christ. Because of what Christ has done on the cross, this radically changes our every day prayer lives. Not only does this transform our prayers individually, but it also transforms prayer in our friendships.

When you approach the throne of God to make a request for you or a friend the Christian is able to take comfort in the fact that his request will be heard because he is praying in Christ and through the Spirit. When a friend asks you to pray for him on a given issue and you do not know what to pray, the Spirit intercedes for you and takes it to the Father. We do not have to have the anxiety of worrying, "Am I praying or saying the right things that need to be said?" Sanders once again is helpful in showing the freedom from anxiety when coming to the Lord in prayer when he says,

> *We are invited to enter that eternal conversation in an appropriately lower, creaturely way, but the heavenly analogue of prayer is already going on in the life of God rather than waiting for us to get it started. If you have ever become weary of working up the right response in prayer or*

worship, you can glimpse the relief of being able to approach prayer and worship with the knowledge that the party already started before you arrived.[43]

You don't have to feel the awkwardness of being the first guy to the party, which the host has to entertain until everyone gets there. There are no need for ice-breakers or "how about the weather" conversations. The Gospel Transformed Friendship is given a glorious freedom of knowing that he may not have the right words to say and he may not know all the details, but he is able to join into a conversation that has been going on since eternity. He is able to join this conversation without fear of judgment. He is also given the comfort of knowing that God will give an ear to his request because of what Christ has done on his behalf. The Gospel Transformed Friendship prays through Christ and for others. The Gospel Transformed friendship has a prayer life that is not individualistic, but is focused on advancing the kingdom of God in the whole body of Christ. One of the best ways to pray for and with others is to pray through the Psalms. The church historically has used the book of Psalms as a model for prayer. Praying through the Psalms is a wonderful way to learn to pray for others.

---

[43] Ibid, 215.

PRAYER IN THE GARDEN TEMPLE

A trap that Christians often fall guilty of when praying through the Psalms, is only praying for the ones that are relevant to their lives at that particular time. Christians pray Psalms about suffering when they are going through hard times. When times are good they pray through Psalms of thanksgiving. The beauty of praying the Psalms with others is that it forces you to pray Psalms about suffering (lament) even when things are going well. I am not suggesting that we be a morbid people that are constantly thinking about the negative. What I am suggesting is that praying these sort of Psalms makes our friends' sufferings our suffering. This forces us to change the way that we pray from "I' and "me" prayers to "we" and "our" prayers. Praying the Psalms together makes your friend's trials and heartaches, your trials and heartaches. Once the gospel takes root in our lives it changes the way that we pray for others. One of the best places to see other-focused prayers is in the Puritans.

The Puritans always find the perfect way to put a book's worth of information into one sentence. It seemed to me that if a Puritan writer ever felt like there was more that needed to be said on a subject, he would just add a comma and tack on another paragraph at the end of his current sentence. John Bunyan, one of my favorite Puritan writers, demonstrates this quality when defining prayer. Bunyan defines prayer as,

PRAYER IN THE GARDEN TEMPLE

A sincere, sensible, affectionate pouring out of the heart or soul to God, through Christ, in the strength and assistance of the Holy Spirit, for such things as God has promised, or according to his Word, for the good of the church, with submission in faith to the will of God.[44]

Bunyan is helpful is showing how prayer in the Gospel Transformed Friendship is through Christ and is focused on the body as whole. The Gospel Transformed Friendship's prayer life is not focused on building up his or her own personal 401k, house, or car. Prayer is also not a meeting with a physician or a health clinic visit. Prayer was meant to be a means of communicating with the Lord for the purpose of advancing his kingdom throughout the whole earth. When you pray for your friends, are you praying only for their health and wealth, or are you praying for them to have opportunities to share the gospel with their coworkers and friends? Are you praying for God to receive greater glory in your friend's lives with the things that God has already given them (e.g., possessions, health, and job)? John Piper provides a helpful analogy to describe how many

---

[44] John Bunyan, *Pray* (Carlisle: PA, Banner of Truth Trust, 1965), 13.

Christians treat prayer in contrast how the bible describes prayer when he says,

> *The number one reason why prayer malfunctions in the hands of a believers is that they try to turn a wartime walkie-talkie into a domestic intercom. Until you believe that life is war, you cannot know what prayer is for. Prayer is for the accomplishment of a wartime mission...And what did they do with the walkie-talkie? They tried to rig it up as an intercom in their cushy houses and cabins and boats and cars —not to call in fire power for conflict with a mortal enemy, but to ask the maid to bring another pillow to the den.*[45]

The Gospel Transformed Friendships sees prayer not as a means of building up each other's own personal kingdoms, but as a tool for advancing the name of Christ. A friendship that has been transformed by the gospel prays to advance the mission God gave to Adam and Eve in the Garden. God's mission has always been for the entire earth to be filled with His glory. Prayer then acts as a means of accomplishing this goal. A walkie-talkie

---

[45] John Piper, "The Work of Missions" cited at http://www.desiringgod.org/conference-messages/prayer-the-work-of-missions

as Piper suggests is for the purpose of helping accomplish a mission. When you for or with our friends which end of the analogy do your prayers best align? Has sin infiltrated your prayer life and changed your focus? Gospel transformed friendships take back their prayer lives and reclaim them for the name of Christ.

Start reclaiming your prayer life by devoting 10 minutes a night to praying for gospel opportunities in your friends' lives. Pray that the Lord will help them make use of the things, which He has already graciously given to them. While praying with your friends, comfort your friends with a reminder that the Lord does hear their prayer because of what Christ has done. If your friends believe that their prayers are going upon deaf ears or not moving past the ceiling because of mistakes that they have made in the past, remind them that Christ is their righteousness and because of him they can enter the presence of the Lord without fear of judgment. Christ has been judged for their sins, so that they can bring their needs to the Lord. Remind them that they are heard not because of their good works, but because of Christ. A prayer life that has been transformed by the gospel is one, which is not focused on one's self, but is one that is focused on building up Christ's church. Christ died for his bride, the church, because of his love for her (Ephesians 5:25) Therefore, we should give our lives, especially our prayer lives, to loving the church as well (Ephesians 5:1). Pray for and with your friends that the love, grace, and mercy of Christ may flourish within your friendships.

APPLICATION

1. How does prayer relate to the temple? (DISCUSS)

2. Why is it significant that Christians pray through Christ? (DISCUSS)

3. How does the gospel change the way in which we pray for our friends? (DISCUSS)

4. Get together with a friend this week and spend time with them in prayer. (PLAN)

5. Pray this week that God will advance His kingdom purposes in the lives of your friends. (PLAN)

6. Read through and pray through Luke 11 with a friend. (READ)

ABOUT THE AUTHOR

Adam Holland resides in Knoxville, Tn with his wife, Katelyn, and their children – Emma Kate, Isaiah Caedmon, and Scarlett Eden. He is the pastor of Hope Church of Knoxville. He graduated from Boyce College (B.A.) and the Southern Baptist Theological Seminary (M. Div.). He is the author of the book of "Friendship Redeemed." Adam frequently writes articles and reviews for several different online, newspaper, and magazine publications.

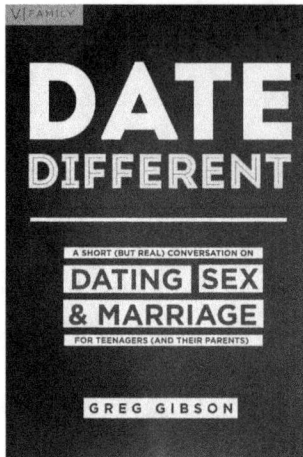

When Jesus saves us, everything changes. If we understand this, then our practice of dating, sex, and marriage simply cannot stay the same. The logic is pretty clear. Jesus saves us. Jesus changes us. Jesus changes how we view and practice things. Dating is one of those things. Sex is one of those things. Marriage is one of those things. Let's begin a conversation about how Jesus calls us to... Date Different.

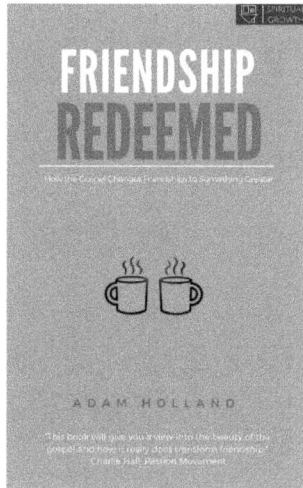

Friendship Redeemed is an examination of how the gospel influenced and shaped Paul's understanding of friendship. Pastors, students, and teachers alike —and anyone who desires to grow in their understanding of biblical friendship—will find this work to be a helpful resource, both in regards to readability and substance. Friendship Redeemed examines the topic of friendship through the lens of the metanarrative of scripture. The conclusion is that the gospel calls the Christian to a unique and counter-cultural view of friendship. This book will serve as a tool for helping believers to learn to live and think with a biblical worldview concerning the topic of friendship.